CAREER GUIDE

HOW TO BE A PROFESSIONAL

BASIC ART AND BUSINESS ANSWERS ON A CAREER AS A PROFESSIONAL LINE ARTIST IN ADVERTISING AND MASS COMMUNICATIONS

RUTH CORBETT

ART DIRECTION BOOK COMPANY
NEW YORK, NEW YORK

To T. Montgomery Orr, an art director who was a pleasure to work with because he knew what he wanted and could explain the job understandably.
R.C.

Copyright © 1988 Ruth Corbett
All rights reserved
Printed in the United States of America

No part of this book may be reproduced, stored in a retrieval system, or transmitted in any form by any means, electronic, mechanical, photocopying, recording or otherwise, without the prior permission of the publishers.

ISBN: 0-88108-045-4 (Cloth)
0-88108-046-2 (Paper)

Library of Congress Catalog Card No.: 87-72469

Designed by Al Lichtenberg, Lichtenberg/Graphic

Published by Art Direction Book Company
10 East 39th Street
New York, NY 10016

Contents

INTRODUCTION:
    The Importance of Line Art   4

I. MEDIUMS AND TOOLS
    1. Pencil and Charcoal   7
    2. Pen and Ink   15
    3. Accessories   23
    4. Pastel as Line   27

II. METHODS
    5. Working Drawings   33
    6. Ways With Scratchboard   37
    7. Cartoons and Caricatures   45
    8. Spot and Merchandise Art   61
    9. Line and Food   67
    10. Free Lines Wander   73
    11. Line Portraits   79
    12. Combining Line With Tone   91
    13. Stippling Returns   95

III. THE BUSINESS OF LINE ART
    14. What Art Directors Buy   101
    15. An Artist's Line Experiences   115

Acknowledgments   125

Introduction

Line art is one of many branches of art worthy of its own special consideration. Although it may seem too simple alongside the exciting full-color painted illustrations, line art has many modes and moods of expression and will show up cleanly in many places (such as newsprint) where full-color art will not. The cost of preparation and reproduction are also significantly greater with full-color art.

These considerations immediately make line art take an important spot in ad art. Lines may be handled in myriad ways, not only in black and white, but also in colored pencil, ink, dye and paint.

It behooves illustrators to polish line techniques along with other forms of art if they wish to have well-rounded portfolios. Whether you aspire to a steady staff job or the more "sky's the limit" free-lance adventure, you must examine how broadly and well your samples will represent you. Do they show you at your best and most versatile?

Some art directors moan that they see so little line art so you should learn the craft if you haven't, sprinkling line art generously among your full-color "prizes" that may have gotten you nowhere so far.

First, be certain you can draw. This may sound facetious to artists with professional status, but if art directors stress this point, they must see many examples to the contrary. Don't carry around a batch of apologies which always beg for alibis. These could punch you out before you're started.

Explore all of the techniques shown or explained here and you'll eventually develop a style of your own – a way of handling line mediums – as distinctive as your own signature.

6 *MEDIUMS AND TOOLS*

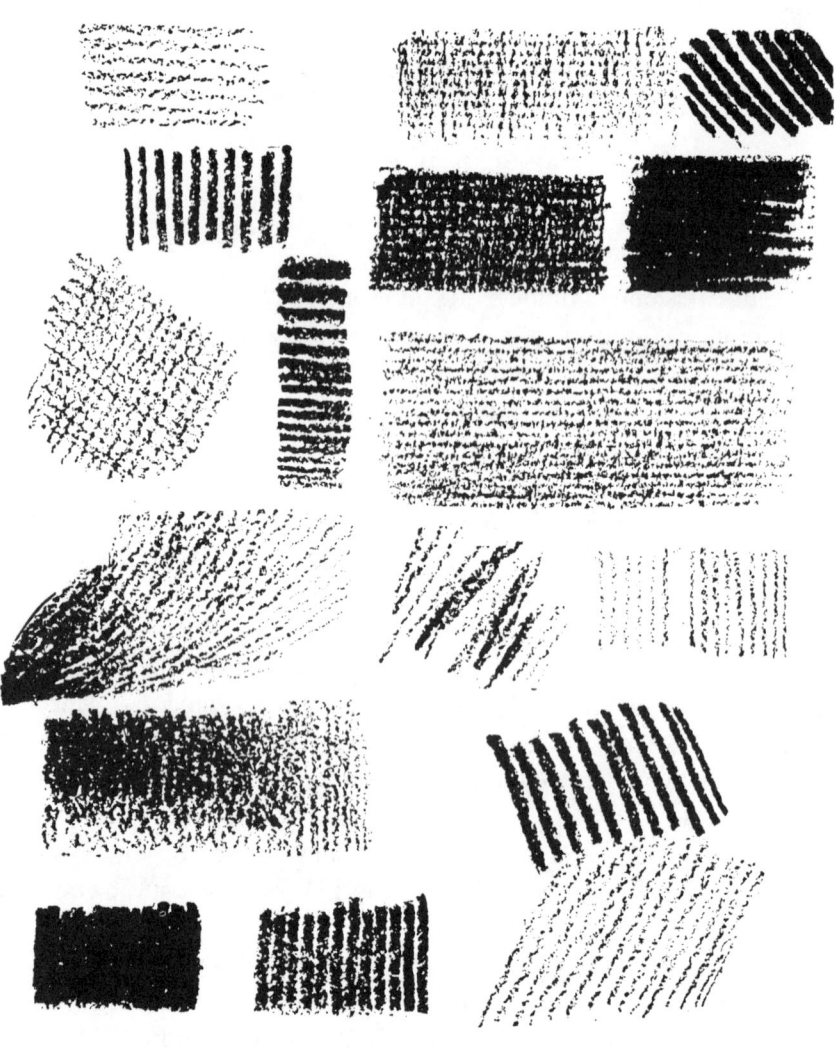

Pencil and charcoal practice swatches.

I / MEDIUMS AND TOOLS

1
Pencil and Charcoal

Pencil is about as basic as a drawing material can get, but there are so many varieties from which to choose. Which is best? It's largely dependent on the kind of job at hand plus the look that's preferred. A graphite pencil generally gives a drier, more linear drawing than other line mediums.

For some subjects it's preferable to have the solid deep rich blacks of soft Wolff pencils which run in six degrees from HH (very hard) to BBB (extra black and soft), and four graduated grades between. I like Wolff pencils because they cling better and do less "dusting off" than charcoal. Each artist develops individual tastes in all materials used (thank goodness we don't still have to wrestle with dusty vine stick charcoal as I did in school art class), too much emphasis can't be made about practice swatches for all mediums. The better you're acquainted with all types of line-makers, the more clean-cut and effortless the resulting drawings will appear.

Another helpful practice is carrying a small pocket or purse-sized sketch pad and sketch pencils of whichever grades and sort you prefer. Don't just tote them around, but get the habit of quick line sketches wherever you can fit in a few moments of observations of all interesting people or objects you see. Free models are everywhere, although they only pose in one position a few minutes. This may seem like an elementary suggestion, but it could be likened to a virtuoso who still practices on the instrument daily.

8 Wolff pencil in several grades was used entirely for all lines and tones. (Author's illustration for her book, *Mama Played Mah-Jongg*.)

A large-leaded graphite pencil and sketch pad was on hand when I visited historic Glory Hole Bar in Central City, Colorado.

10 MEDIUMS AND TOOLS

Such sketches may only be readable to the artist, but they are good for the experience of making quick notes from what you see. This effort isn't too much trouble or wasted time if an artist has serious ambitions. When it comes to turning doodling into dollars, spare no effort.

With sufficient practice a line drawing can show as much comprehension of a subject as a highly polished painting, not even lacking color if colored pencils are used. These could be crayon-like pencils or pastel.

Charming line effects can be obtained with sanguine or sepia Conté crayons. For portraits their effect is softer and warmer than black, especially if they're to be framed works. Of course, black will reproduce better as a rule.

One pencil no artist should be without is the All-Stabilo graphite pencil. It will mark on all surfaces, and although you may not do a lot of marking on chinaware, you might well do so on glossy photo prints. It gives a rich black on paper and yet is erasable.

Charcoal pencil on a moderately toothy paper. (Book illustration by author for her book, *Mama Played Mah-Jongg*.)

A litho pencil is good for fast sketches out in the field. They have rich blacks and need no fixative.

12 MEDIUMS AND TOOLS

A broad Negroid lead in a grip holder made this quick sketch from life on a pad suitable for pencil, charcoal or water-based paint.

The charcoal encased in wood can hardly be entirely avoided if you're in any way connected with black-and-white layout-making. A working artist should be equipped with several grades of charcoal as well as Wolff carbon pencils. Another necessity is the easily-applied Blaisdell China marker. It's wrapped in paper, is self-sharpening (by peeling the paper away from the worn point), and can be indispensable for photo markups for the engraver.

Another useful tool is the lithographic (or "litho") pencil. I've often used it when sketching out in the field because the blacks are good and need no fixative as with charcoal, Wolff or pastel. It's good to travel as lightly as possible when sketching on location. For good texture of litho line, I like a moderately-toothed sketch paper.

Other items for the equipment cabinet would be thick-leaded drafting pencils to work in any detail in conjunction with graphite sticks to get broad effects on layouts – whether on tissue or bond layout pads. These help speed jobs which are always wanted in a rush.

It's not amiss to have a set of Prismacolor pencils on hand, especially when fine color detailing is needed. These require no fixing. Some artists like to have a set of Faber-Castell water-soluble color pencils for either field sketching or use in the studio where both line and wash effects are wanted.

A good time-saver for many artists is a lead holder. You simply press a button at the top of the shaft to project the lead. Chucks grip the lead firmly with no slipping. For the one made by Morilla, refill leads come in thirteen grades from H to 6B. Several other brands are also obtainable.

A number of accessories should find taboret space among the array of pencils, pens and brushes. Especially needed are sandpaper blocks, not only for pointing-up pencils, but for sharpening the frisket knife edge. You may also find other uses.

If you can convince an art director to provide an electric pencil sharpener, you're in luck. However, you may prefer to hand-sharpen the wood to expose a longer lead, then point the end on a sandpaper block. It's advisable to have a package of single-edge razor blades. They're also good for under-angle-cutting of photos if you're asked to assemble photo parts.

Don't forget an assortment of erasers and frisket knives. A much-used eraser in my work is a pencil-and-ink eraser pencil. They're best for removing small hard-to-get spots. And no artist should be without a ruby eraser and kneadable rubber. The fact that the latter leaves no crumbs is a big plus.

14 MEDIUMS AND TOOLS

Pen and ink was used for the drawing and charcoal made the tone. (Author's illustration for her book, *Film City and Suburbs.***)**

2
Pen and Ink

When we mention line art, most artists and non-artists immediately think of pen and ink. Lines may be drawn with any medium, but crisp black ink on white paper is still the most important branch of line art. There are endless possibilities in the ways pens and brushes may be wielded when filled with the richness of India ink.

Because of their steel flexibility, I've always liked the little crowquill pen point and its small hardwood or plastic holder. Another favorite is the larger point of the versatile Gillott's #290, a flexible point producing lines which swell smoothly from fine to wide, depending on the pressure exerted. Other Gillott pens have variations in stiffness, and the stiffest can make more uniform lines without flexing.

A family of pens which shouldn't be neglected are the fiber-tipped ones. Some artists swear by these, especially for sketching in the field. They are available in varying sizes and widths as well as intensities of tone. When Pentel pens first appeared, some layout men switched entirely to these for layout renderings instead of the graphite or charcoal pencils formerly used. This was because of their speed, clear fleshy tones which dry instantly and require no fixing. It's been my experience that practice is needed for these, and once down, they aren't erasable. They will soak through some kinds of paper, especially bond layout pad paper. When using the juicier wide tips, this soaking tendency should be checked first on the paper to be used. They slide easily onto tissue without bleed-through, then show up well if the tissue is mounted with staples onto white stock.

16   MEDIUMS AND TOOLS

Pen and ink practice swatches.

    The amount of ink in the fiber-tipped pens can affect the width or texture of line obtained. Nice tonal effects can be made when ink in the pen is nearly all used. This encourages the artist to get full mileage from each pen one way or another.

    The array of quick-drying, permanent, fade-proof ink-in-pens of all types has proliferated to an almost confusing number. Trying "one of each" is the best suggestion I could make. This was the way I picked those most useful for my work.

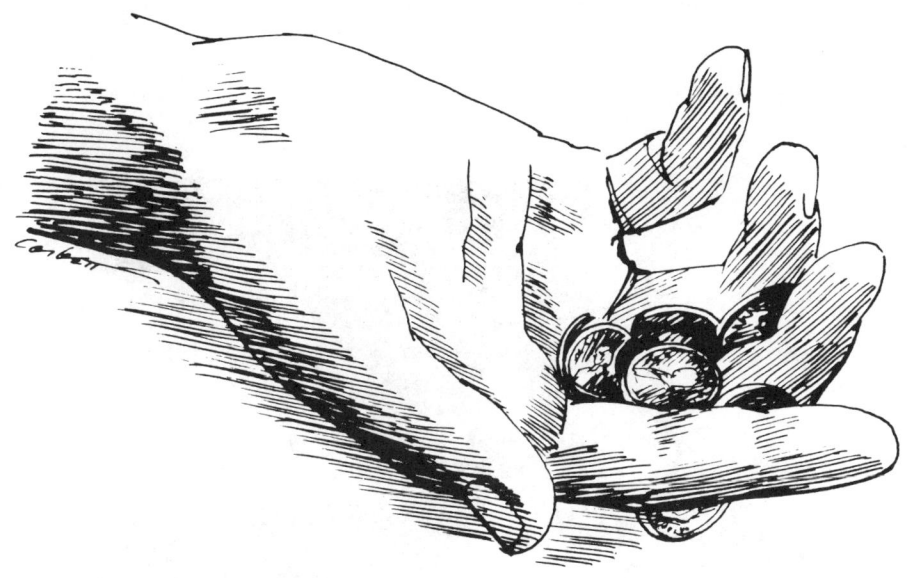

Flexible pen nibs produce lines of varying thickness, giving the art a lively appearance.

Black silhouettes can effectively show all that's needed for some ideas. Little detail is necessary.

18   MEDIUMS AND TOOLS

An example of the many techniques achievable with fine points on technical pens. Solids pull it together. (Courtesy Provident Federal Savings)

No truer words could be said: even in line drawing each medium has its own peculiar properties. This is surely true when pen-and-ink drawings are considered. For instance, Pigma Pens have all of the foregoing qualities of drying and permanence plus clean non-feathering lines that neither smear nor bleed through paper. You can even brush water-based paints over with no blurring. The lines flow smoothly and evenly for satisfactory results. They come in sets of three widths in the package.

Tombow has gone a step farther by making one implement serve two purposes. It's dual brush-pen, double-tipped for medium or bold

There's no limitation on subject matter for the fine metal points. (Courtesy S. Thompson Adverstising, Salt Lake City, Utah.)

strokes with fast-drying, water-base odorless ink (with a choice of 72 colors). A fiber tip at one end provides fine lines. On the other end is a brush which when dipped in water can spread color where wanted.

In today's line art world, artists can't ignore the impact made by Koh-I-Noor Rapidograph technical pens. Thirteen line widths are obtainable, with the tubular nib allowing movement in any direction on almost any surface. The refillable ink cartridges ensure that long drawing sessions needn't be interrupted by running out of ink or the need to keep dipping the point in a bottle. There's no end to the techniques this pen encourages with ease. Present popularity of ink "pointillism" is probably due to the Rapidograph pen's facile dot capability with varied point sizes.

Koh-I-Noor distributes another breakthrough product for line art from sketching to calligraphy – the Rotring Art Pen. Its talents lie in the variety of nibs, including flexible ones which vary line widths with hand pressure changes, along with smooth, sweeping lines. The fine stainless steel nibs are hand-finished for precision quality. The Rotring Art Pen uses pre-filled black ink cartridges.

There is something to be said in favor of keeping an open mind about pens, as well as other aspects of line drawing. Just as you're well-practiced and accustomed to one kind of instrument, something new and/or revolutionary will appear. Try them all if possible.

20 MEDIUMS AND TOOLS

Effective use of solids, lines and crosshatch give full tonality to this bird with feathers nicely detailed. (Courtesy of artist William S. Tilton, *The Artists* Magazine.)

The simple directness give this illustration modern effectiveness.

Control gained by humble practice is the key to pen and ink. I suggest making various kinds of practice swatches, using hatching, crosshatching and stippling to make a series of tones from black to white. Take a finely pointed steel pen, perhaps a crowquill, and fairly smooth but not shiny paper and black waterproof India ink. Lay lines quickly (slowly-drawn lines show it), making patches with different line widths and distances apart. Then try crosshatching at various angles over the underlying lines – first at right angles, then diagonally toward the right and left. This gives a good texture for clothing material and has enough light flecks to be distinguished from solid black.

After a good amount of such practice, you will gain confidence with the tool until the results are quickly done but under complete control. With faithful practice you should become able to draw lines toward you or away, from right or left, while still having control. On some jobs it's mighty handy to not have to keep turning the board because you can only draw in one direction.

3
Accessories

What are the virtues of good ink? It should have a dense black tone, flow freely from all pens, be waterproof and reasonably fast drying. It should adhere to the board or paper without clogging or having uneven flowing qualities. There are many makers, but some well-known names are Higgins, Pelikan and Koh-I-Noor.

A bit needs to be said about pen cleaners and the absolute necessity of keeping pen points clean. This is especially true if you expect to keep technical pens in working order. The major ink makers also offer pen cleaning solutions. It's good to have soft cloth or a box of tissues nearby to frequently wipe points so ink never gets a chance to dry on them.

Probably the worst case of unclean pens were those used by an artist with whom I once worked. Each of his pen points was encased by a hardened ball of ink with about one-sixteenth-inch of point showing. Offhand, I'd say *none* of his pens were flexible. With technical pens, tender care is particularly imperative if they're to work as intended.

Another accessory a line artist shouldn't be without is an assortment of erasers. Yes, erasing ink is possible – but it's not easy. I've had excellent results on good quality illustration board where ink removal is desired. First the ink area is gently scraped with a single-edge razor blade held at an angle. Don't press too hard so as to cut or otherwise harm the surface. If the area is too small for the razor blade, a variety of small X-Acto blades are available.

24 MEDIUMS AND TOOLS

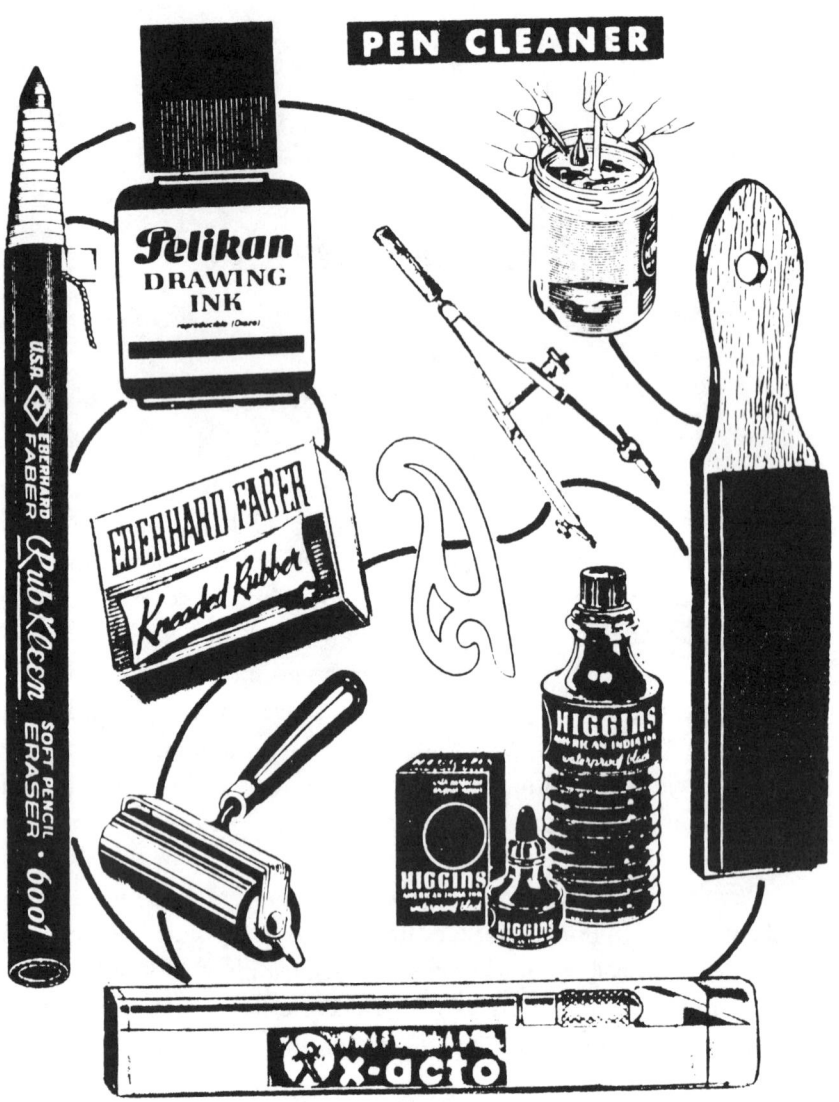

Standard accessories for advertising artists.

Accessories   25

The technique for the race horses takes considerable reduction well. (Courtesy J.B. Deneen, illustrator, represented by Joe Mendola, NYC. Art in *TV Guide*.)

Use a soft brush to gently remove ink and paper dust after the scraping. An ink eraser pencil should then be firmly but gently circled around the area being changed. The final act is to rub over the spot with a kneaded rubber. This whole operation is the reason for using a board of excellent quality and weight whenever possible: it can withstand ink removal and be workable with the pen and ink afterward.

Kneaded rubber is practically indispensable because it's gentle, it absorbs marks and leaves no crumbs. (I'll never forget the shower of crumbs from Artgum erasers in school art classes.) Ruby and Pink Pearl rubber erasers are good for general erasures, particularly of pencil underdrawings when rendering in pen and ink.

The wonderful eraser pencils – a soft grade for pencil erasing and a grittier grade for ink – are paper-wound for self-freshening. They're useful in small spaces where other erasers would be too large and clumsy.

You may collect other pet tools and accessories as you go along, but these are the basic essentials. Don't forget to cap bottles of India ink when not in use, wipe pens and otherwise police the taboret top to keep efficiency tip-top. This "housekeeping" pays off in cleaner, faster work without searches for necessary items when needed in a hurry.

Drawing surfaces haven't been mentioned, but my choices may not be yours. When the art is to be reduced and later coupled with other ad components, I prefer a hot-pressed illustration board of good quality. A toothier cold-press finish may be right for some drawings but the pen won't glide over it as smoothly. On the other hand, if art is done separately to be mounted with the rest of the parts, then it can be on unmounted ply paper. A plate finish in a 2-ply Strathmore works well. Some artists like Bristol board for pen and ink, especially for stippled illustrations. As always, individual preference and the nature of a job should dictate.

4
Pastel as Line

When we speak of this medium, it's in a different sense of usage than many would expect. Artists often think of pastel only as a full-color, blended, smoothly toned effect on velour paper or sanded pastel board. But it may also be used as a line medium, applied as distinct line strokes without blending, except as our eyes do it for us.

There are several types of pastel quite unlike each other. We usually think of this material as sticks in a wide range of colors, but they also come in a good range of greys from black to white. My sets of greys were made in Austria by Koh-I-Noor Pencil Company and distributed in the United States by L. & C. Hardmuth of Bloomsbury, New Jersey. The set includes eight square sticks which may be used as a layout medium as well as for illustrations.

Carbo-Othello hard pastels are made in Germany in a range of sixty colors. They're quarter-inch square sticks, easy to apply, neat to use and with a minimum of powdering. They're quite widely used for commercial art jobs.

Several of my other pastel sets are round sticks designated as soft. Of course, each manufacturer claims superiority for their product. In a set of forty non-fading sunproof colors, Grumbacher uses no fugitive colors in the quest for permanence of artists' work. The boxes come in a general selection, for landscapes, or geared to portraiture. Portraits are one of the main uses for pastels.

28 MEDIUMS AND TOOLS

Pastel line practice swatches.

Alphacolor sets have forty-eight square sticks of unusually soft, smooth, brilliant hues – some being fluorescent color. These are made by Weber Costello. They're usable for sketching on all types of paper (except enameled stock), illustration board or even canvas.

Although most companies offer sets of various colors, some have only enough for beginners. The brands mentioned are but a few of the many available. Smooth velvety qualities are desirable for ease of use with minimum dust-off.

Pastel as Line

Black and white pastel with three greys in between.

What paper is appropriate for drawing with pastel line strokes? Illustration boards, minimum rough or a hard surface will take pastel and charcoal. Of course, pastel lines can be laid on sanded pastel paper and the surface holds the medium firmly. Another compatible material is charcoal paper. It should be white for commercial jobs. For portraits as wall pictures, I prefer Canson grey paper. When tacking it onto the drawing board, I put several layers of paper beneath for padding. Newspaper will do for this. Canson pastel and charcoal

On a toothy board surface pastel sticks worked for the vertical line technique.

papers come in 33 colors. This company should know what they're doing since they've been paper makers since 1157 A.D., and few manufacturers of anything can make such a claim.

Pastel as Line **31**

To avoid smudging the pastel lines, spray lightly with workable fixative while drawing and when the work is finished.

Unlike soft pastels, the oil pastels are dust-free and hard to smudge. These sticks can be used on paper, board or canvas and give the effect of oil color. Because of the oily binder which holds the pigment particles together, they're not as fragile as soft pastel and require no fixative.

A charcoal pencil was used here and gave rich solids while pastel color sticks furnished the other tones. (Author's illustration for her book, *Gone Forever Again.***)**

32 MEDIUMS AND TOOLS

This complicated New York brownstone scene was a layout working rendering with charcoal pencil, greatly reduced. Drawn on tracing tissue.

II / METHODS

5
Working Drawings

While all drawing is "work," we're interested here in the preliminary steps which keep the final line art surface from looking like a disaster area. Excessive smearing and erasure should be avoided on the illustration board or paper meant for the finished work.

Working drawings are made on a tissue pad, also called tracing paper pad. It's quite transparent, smooth and surprisingly tough when repeatedly erased. All of the changes of intent, mistakes and thinking-on-paper should be on these tissues, resulting in a thoroughly accurate pencil line delineation of the subject for final rendering.

There are a number of ways to transfer the drawing onto the final board or paper. For many years I used a wide graphite stick to rub on the back of the tissue. In this process, the tissue is placed right side up on the illustration board. As you carefully trace over your drawing, the graphite on the back of the tissue will transfer onto the board. It was a fast and satisfactory procedure. But later came the luxury of having already prepared, precision-made transfer paper, available in rolls or flat sheets. Laid between the tissue drawing and finished surface, it produces a sharp, delicate line without a trace of dusting or greasiness. It's erasable with kneaded rubber or soft Ruby. Although it comes in several colors of transfer backing, graphite is best for commercial work. For the tracing-down I use a sharply pointed 8H or 9H Venus pencil which acts like a stylus but is less likely to cut through the tissue than a metal stylus.

34 METHODS

On these working drawings I usually indicate lines for the shadow pattern, such as on faces and figures, occasionally filling in the shadows so the overall tonality can be seen before putting the drawing on the finishing surface. It gives a better guide to the drawing's finished appearance. The complete shadow areas are not transferred, however — only the outlines of the shadow areas.

It's good practice to have a file or envelope in which to keep the tissue working drawings. You may need them again if changes are wanted or the work needs redoing. Yes, this lamentably happens.

Develop the habit of making working drawings. A few tries should demonstrate the advisability of cultivating it into a permanent working practice for advertising art.

Three working tissues, each being more detailed and accurate. (Courtesy Mrs. Agnes Briggs for Robert Fawcett Art.)

Working Drawings 35

The final tissue is ready to transfer onto illustration board.
(Courtesy Mrs. Agnes Briggs for Robert Fawcett Art.)

36 *METHODS*

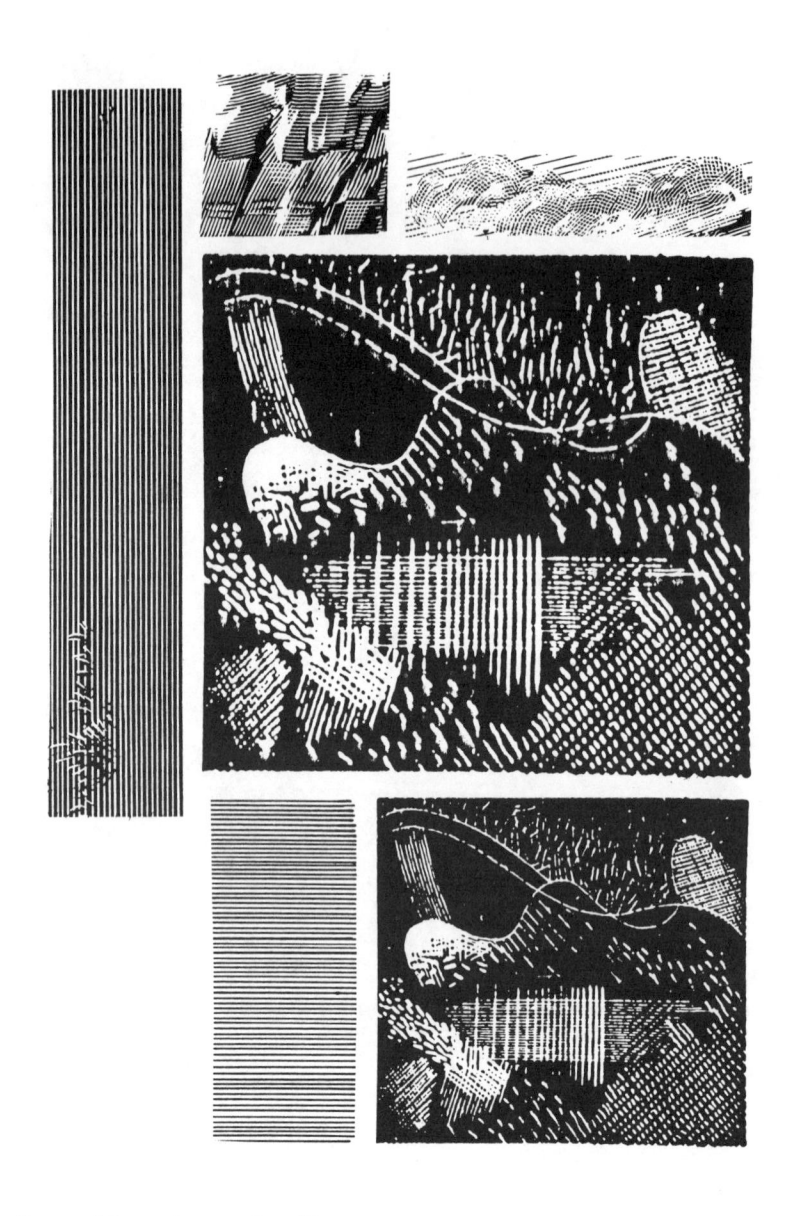

Scratchboard practice lines.

6
Ways with Scratchboard

Don't be surprised if scratchboard drawings fool you into thinking they're woodcuts or steel engravings. They can be mistaken for the earlier mediums for making prints. The effects that can be achieved with scratchboard are numerous, but the artist unfamiliar with it will have to reverse thinking from making black lines on white to making white lines on black.

When you buy scratchboard, get the smooth surfaced type instead of textured board. Whether this covering is labelled "chalk-coated" or "clay-coated," it operates the same way. It is usually a heavy paper instead of a board. Be careful not to bend it at any stage of use because the coating might become cracked. This will ruin everything, especially if a lot of work has already been done.

If you intend to make several separate drawings from one full sheet, carefully cut off and mount only the size needed for each drawing instead of wrestling with the whole sheet. The mounting anchors the scratchboard so it can't curl, ripple or be less than entirely smooth. Lay an even coat of rubber cement on the mount and on the scratchboard's back side. Let both sides cemented dry thoroughly before adhering the two together.

Scratchboard couldn't be called temperamental but is isn't compatible with heavy humidity. Under such atmospheric conditions it doesn't scratch cleanly or easily. What to do? Application of gentle heat – such as a few minutes in a very low-heat oven – could dry it enough to improve line control. Unused sheets should be stored flat in a dry place.

A fine example of varied scratchboard line treatments.

(Courtesy of T.M. Orr.)

This bold scratchboard treatment resembles woodcut or linocut print. It would reproduce well even if substantially reduced in size. (Courtesy T.M. Orr.)

Ways With Scratchboard **41**

Compare this treatment with the other similar figure. Study the subtle handling of muscles and details. (Courtesy of T.M. Orr.)

Any sharply pointed tool can be used to scratch lines into the inked surface, and you may already have some implements in your taboret which will work. The scratching tools made by Hunt resemble drawing pen nibs. A frisket knife of any of several styles could be useful. Some artists have begged an old set of tools from their friendly dentist because these steel implements work well on scratchboard.

If you use uncoated scratchboard, you'll also need good brushes which won't shed hairs in the midst of applying a thin, even coat of India ink. Such imperfections complicate your job.

If this is your first experience with scratchboard, it would be well to first make a series of black squares or rectangles on a small piece of board on which to scratch practice swatches. You may then familiarize yourself with the feel and variety of effects obtainable with various tools. Try rows of straight and curved parallel lines, dots, zigzags and several kinds of crosshatching. Such diverse materials as coarse steel wool, deftly pulled or jabbed on the ink coat, can make unusual and useful textures.

Before you proceed, the drawing should be carefully planned in advance. If your subject has sizable white areas, it would be better to leave the white board for them instead of having to scrape it all out; don't apply ink to areas of the drawing which will remain white.

To proceed in an orderly manner, an outline of the subject should be lightly transferred to the white board as a guide for where to paint the black ink. It could be drawn in pencil first on a tissue like a "working drawing." (Graphite drawings may also be transferred onto black, pre-coated scratchboard, though the lines may be harder to see.)

To start the actual work, remember that scratchboard doesn't well endure erasures or alterations once you're into the scratching. When cutting, always pull the lines toward you – not away. The tool should be held naturally as one would hold a writing implement. The board should be occasionally turned to ensure that lines are drawn toward you.

Don't try to scratch long, unwieldy lines because the hand should always be held so perfect control can be kept. Naturally, the appearance of a line is determined by the kind of tool as well as the artist's way of handling it.

This masterful rendition of Adolphe Menjou shows the subtleties possible in scratchboard. (Courtesy of T.M. Orr.)

Whether the whole surface is blackened beforehand depends on the subject. This is where the necessary pre-planning enters. Scratchboard art generally should have more black than white since contrast is the charm of this medium. Already blackened scratchboard can be bought.

Scratchboard can be used for strikingly clean clarity, especially for glass or silverware. (Courtesy Riedel Crystal of America, Inc.)

You wouldn't draw a basically white subject on a white scratchboard. It would be as punchy as a mashed potato sandwich. In some cases there may be white areas in which it's easier to add a few ink pen lines than to cut all around to leave narrow black lines.

Another point worth remembering is the source of light. It affects the entire look of a scratchboard drawing. Never forget the power of sharp blacks. The light and dark not only give the shapes of objects, but add punch. This makes the medium particularly fine for silverware, glass, jewelry, aluminum kitchenware and all such hard and shiny things.

There are so many individual means of expression in this medium. It can be as individual as your fingerprint. Try all sorts of off-beat approaches. Experiment with effects on the practice swatches and surprise yourself with something beyond the conventional techniques. Be innovative. There are few how-*not*-tos on this subject. Always experiment, even with different ways of applying the black ink to achieve interesting textures. Since we're using only black and white, different treatments are the salvation for this limitation.

7
Cartoons and Caricatures

Nothing is more needed or sought than a chuckle or good healthy guffaw in this world of many cares. Here the cartoonists and caricaturists may flourish in publications where possibly no other artwork is used – and these are usually all or partially line drawings.

It was by chance that I "fell" into this branch of line art while on the staff of a studio handling national advertising accounts. The inclination was strong to say, "No, I don't do cartooning," but I was also reluctant to turn down a job, particularly where there'd be a challenge to try something different.

Exaggeration is the basic difference between straight illustration and cartoons or caricatures. The main features or characteristics are pushed beyond their normal appearance, so a person with a big nose has a bigger one or a scrawny animal is skinnier.

At first glance, this type of line art might appear simplistic, but quite the opposite is true. Before good cartoons or caricatures can be produced, the artist must be an expert draughtsman. Otherwise, without a basic knowledge of the human figure, how can one know where and how to exaggerate its parts? This applies not only to facial features but to action pushed beyond normal. That's the cartoon figure's need. Even a series of quick stick figures can be used effectively to establish a skeleton on which to build the active body.

Think of the differences in faces: bouffant hair, tightly pulled-back, scraggly locks, baldpates, high foreheads or low, apelike ones. Eyes might be large, small, far apart or extremely close, slits or bespectacled. The mouths: wide, thin-lipped, thick, turned up creating side lines or turned down in a sad or sour expression. Men can be bearded, mustached or clean-shaven. Noses are particularly objects for overstatement. They might be long, short, puggish, crooked, broken, beakish or like putty blobs. Chins can be bold, long, jutting, underslung, almost missing or double with necks which are long, scrawny, thin, short, thick or turkey-wrinkled.

Of course, when putting together a cartoon head, facial expressions are the most important and take such forms as: laughter, hilarity, smug smirks, disgust, anger, wonder, fright, horror, crying, frowning, sneering and puzzled.

Some artists (particularly in illustration or fashion art) try to hide their models' hands to avoid drawing them. In all forms of comic line art, however, the hands need to show, to help express emotional actions. The shape and position of the hand and fingers may be exaggerated, but underlying must be a thorough familiarity with how to draw the human hand.

The body lends itself to limitless tampering with proportions, parts and positions. There's the male: tall, short, thin, heavy, potbellied, sunken chest, humped back, stiffly straight or sloppily slouched. The female might be: big-bosomed, overweight, flat-chested, pencil slim, hunched over or strutting straight.

Both men and women may show legs and feet in a variety of ways: bowed, plump, muscled, thin, knock-kneed, shapely, knobby or like pipe stems. The feet may be pudgy, with simple shoes, heeled or flat, large or painfully small to suggest a woman's vanity. The heels may be run-over or no more than unstylish blobs at the ends of pole-straight legs.

A cartoonist or any artist who distorts a drawing must first know what the conventional look is. Here's another good argument for carrying a sketch pad and not forgetting why you have it. It's also a strong case for building a clipping file. Mine is dog-eared from much use, and is the fourth one I've built – not for copying styles, but just to know how a wide range of things look and are made.

Objects for dressing sets in which characters live, move and perform should be drawn quite simply in outline, sometimes lighter than main human figures so as not to dominate the scene. Solid blacks in any parts should be laid in with brushes instead of pen; it's hard on pen points, slow and sometimes roughens paper surfaces.

Cartoons and Caricatures 47

The extremely individual style of Norm Bendell cartoons. (Represented by David Goldman Agency.)

48 METHODS

There's a ready market for exaggerated cartoonish illustration in line. It should be

Cartoons and Caricatures **49**

story-telling as this is. (© Samuel B. Whitehead, artist, *Writer's Digest*, Sept. 1986)

1. Short Neck
2. Slim Features
3. Too Broad Face
4. Worn-weary Look
5. Small Eyes
6. Lack of Charm
8. Long narrow Face

7. Awkward Walk

9. Broad Shoulders

50 A single pen line was enough for these cartoon expressions and figures.

A charcoal pencil gave the broad, bold blacks appropriate to the subject. (Author's cartoon for her book, *Film City and Suburbs*.)

Animals offer as many action possibilities as people. Their actions can be intensified by skid lines for fast stops, short straight or curved lines can suggest scratching, puzzlement, jumping, barking for dogs or hissing cats. If they're jumping or running so fast as to be above ground, scratchy pen lines can show the ground line while a series of straight horizontal lines indicate speed. Of course, animals of all kinds are funny when they express human characteristics. Don't forget, they can have "facial" expressions.

Myrt and Matt

"Matt, can't you let the stock market take care of itself until we have a dip?"

Myrt and Matt

"Has Matt joined the Conservation Corps or Agricultural Club?"
"No, every time he throws out all the junk mail, he mutters then plants another tree."

Myrt and Matt

"Just between us girls, Myrt, don't you think Cora could work a little harder on her long putts?"

"Myrt & Matt," a single-panel continuing cartoon about a retired couple, is drawn with felt-tip pens, at least twice the size printed.

Cartoons and Caricatures **53**

Note how pure blacks lead the eye to the cartoon's point. (Courtesy of Monty Orr.)

All of the foregoing is actually preparation for the most important part – creating a situation, whether in a cartoon strip, sport cartoon, spot cartoon or advertising. Few artists are able to start a strip cartoon for syndication in several hundred newspapers. These have to be blessed with themes, ideas, and clearly defined characters which can continue consistently for years.

Whether in a strip of several panels or a single-panel cartoon – if the same characters continue – the artist must know how they'll look from any angle or position. For this purpose, reference drawings should always be in the artist's file.

A subject some artists aren't wildly fond of when in school is composition, but it's vitally important for cartoonists because each situation, whether in a panel frame or not, requires good composition for its components. This arranging of people in their settings should gradually be built up from rough pencil indications until the final rendering refines it.

Whatever is shown in the single panel should be immediately understandable as a whole story. No matter whether the subject is general humor, political or a sports situation, simple, strong, direct lines are the means to the telling end. Some cartoonists use the attention-getting device of having the principle character in solid black clothing while other figures and background are in outline with lighter effects.

In cartoons, bore through to the main point instead of cluttering with meaningless details. Economy of detail helps more for getting the point across than an elaborate drawing.

To add shaded areas to the line drawing, some artists use crayon, charcoal, wash or a variety of acetate overlay sheets for dots or other pattern tones. Others rely on pen lines to establish tone or set certain elements away from others with solid blacks.

Word balloons are seldom used in modern spot cartoons, but some use hand-lettered blocks at the panel's top or bottom portion within the frame lines. Balloons are mostly for strips to show who's talking.

Political cartooning is a special field all by itself and is a powerful tool to expose situations, unsavory politicians and to influence people's thinking. It might be classed as a medium of satirical exposé which has more thrust than pages of written matter. The early American beginnings of this cartooning branch are credited to Thomas Nast who appeared in *Harper's Weekly* in the 19th century. He was largely responsible for exposing the infamous Boss Tweed and his cohorts. Political cartooning's power lies in briefly but incisively showing a possibly complex situation with simple line art.

Whenever the word "simple" is applied to drawing, it's often confused with simple-minded, but never forget that simplicity can be difficult to achieve. It's usually the result of many eliminations until the main bones of the matter are powerfully revealed.

The famous editorial cartoonist, J.N. "Ding" Darling used a different pen technique in a story about Russia's "Five-Year-Plan" when he visited there. The black area helps the composition.

Lithographic pencil on a pebbled board, along with black ink brushed on for solids and lines in pen, have long been the means for political cartoon expression. It reproduces well in newspapers because crayon on the pebbled board leaves distinct dots which reproduce as halftone areas. In order to make some parts stand away or to bring out important elements, many cartoonists add screen tints in various patterns or dots. Sheets of these tint screens are available at most art supply stores, manufactured by Letraset, Presstype, Formatt and others.

Political cartoonists must have keen observation. They should be able to draw likenesses of well-known people so no labeling is necessary. One cartoonist went all over his city until he could find a steam roller to sketch on the spot for accuracy. All artists should be this conscientious about correctness in all objects they use in a drawing.

Comic drawings for magazines are one of the most-used forms of art still left since photography has eliminated many areas for publication. There's always a market for cartoons which can bring smiles and chuckles to the burdened populace. These periodicals range from frankly humorous magazines to women's, fraternal and club, automotive magazines – to barely touch the periodical market for single-panel cartoons. Any artist who hankers to sell in this vast area, shouldn't labor without a current *Artist's Market*, an annual directory published by Writer's Digest Books. Working without it would be like planting a garden without tools to break the ground. Out of 705 magazines listed in the *Artist's Market*, 400 use cartoons. This should give a clear idea of the number of places a free-lance who can cartoon might make sales.

Since magazine cartoons are customarily printed on finer paper than newspapers, they are often line drawings combined with wash for tonal effects rather than being strictly limited to line. These are also usually in vignette form – floating within the borders of the single panel – rather than extending to fill the entire panel.

While the irregularity of a fading-away shape allows freer treatment, these deceptive drawings are carefully planned with preliminary sketches and studies. There may be three or four distinct steps before the final rendering. Rough thumbnail sketches with a soft pencil can show possible arrangement of elements, tonal effects and center of interest. Next, a harder pencil can draw parts carefully in detailed outline. After this, the lines can be inked. The last step establishes solid blacks and any desired tone. Of course, all cartoonists develop their own methods with experience. Several have chosen to always use only pen outline for all parts with maybe one small spot of black on the lead character to catch the eye. If the drawing is of a rather complicated subject, more skill is needed to make it "read"– to put over the humorous point – when no tone directs the eye.

Many cartoon elements find their way into advertising, though not always as the main selling attraction. You may be called on to do some form of exaggerated drawing of people, animals or inanimate objects. At first this might seem a tough problem, but by experimenting with facial expressions, adding legs and arms to animals or objects, you can develop some lively creations. I was once asked to make human gestures and expressions on bulldogs. At first I balked,

The idea's the thing plus style, to make cartoons that sell. (Norm Bendell, represented by the David Goldman Agency.)

but after trying it I found it could be done quite easily. Make distortion serve your purpose without adding extraneous matter unless that matter *is the point.*

Merchandising can often profit by using some well-directed humor. Potential customers don't like to always be hit in their wallets with sledge hammers. It's pleasanter to buy something after the ribs have been tickled, so many advertisers use judicious amounts of cartoon humor to sell goods.

Consider the number of advertisers who've adopted continuing characters which become recognized as representatives of certain products. Sometimes they're trademark figures readily known for the products they adorn.

Here again, as in all foregoing cartooning, the idea should be roughed into a layout sketch first, then gradually refined. Many artists like to use well-pointing sable brushes with ink instead of the scratchier pen, particularly if the board has a tooth or texture.

Let's suppose you design a cartoon figure for a manufacturer or for any purpose where it's to be used in varying positions. A good

58 METHODS

The flapper is finding her place in history in this ink drawing. (Author's cartoon for her book, *Film City and Suburbs*.)

way to ensure that it always looks like the same character is to model a small figure in clay or other material, so it may be turned in any direction to show how changed positions would look.

Probably everyone has at some time enjoyed identifying the people represented by caricatures. With a few deft, telling lines, the subject's most noticeable features are exaggerated. Some faces are naturally close to caricatures and little exaggeration is needed. The most difficult ones to do are the "beautiful people" who have pretty or handsome regular features, so there aren't outstanding noses or other oddities with which to quickly catch the likeness.

Danzig
Virtually Handed to Hitler While Eyes of the World Were Focused on Wars

Brushed in with lamp black tube watercolor. Hitler was a natural for the caricaturist.

One way to get into such a sketch is to study the head, determine what feature or features are outstanding – let's say a large, crooked nose – then draw that first and develop the rest of the head around it. Also study the wrinkles which contribute to each person's appearance. Heavy jowls, extra chins, ears either unusually large or small, should be noted along with hair characteristics which distinguish the subject.

If the whole body is to be shown, there are plenty of body features which lend themselves to the keen caricaturist's eye. The rotund middle can approach a full circle. Big bosoms are shown larger, and prominent hips are played up along with posture peculiarities. Thickly muscled or stick-slim, bowed or knock-kneed legs are characteristic of some.

Whether or not you intend to pursue cartooning and caricaturing, it's a valuable extra asset to have in your bag of know-how because the editors and art directors who buy such line art will be receptive if you've learned your craft well. The rewards can be considerable for becoming a good rib-tickler.

A line artist never knows what request will come next. In this case a clipping file helped for reference.

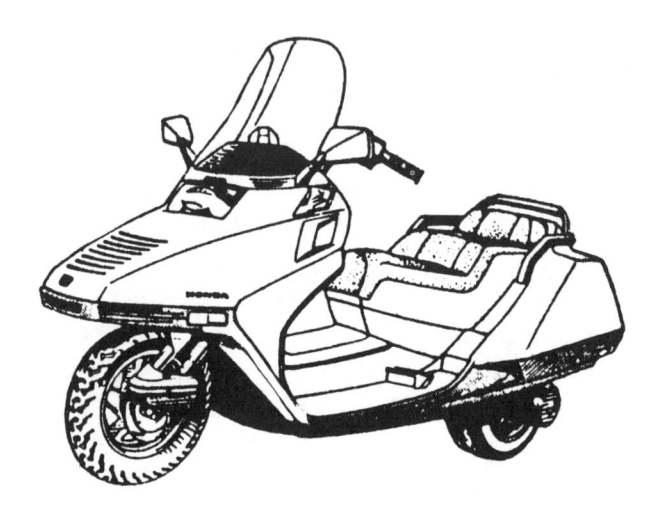

Pen lines may need only to be simple outlines of merchandise to do the necessary selling job.

8
Spot and Merchandise Art

There must be as many uses for spot and merchandise art as there are lakes in Minnesota. Thousands. This is why it pays to polish your skills and the handling of line art in whatever medium. If you wish to be in the admirable class known as "employed artists," this is a good route toward that goal.

Line art can be used to brighten otherwise heavy, overwhelming blocks of type in an ad. It can show the products and demonstrate their use. Spot art can coax potential customers to stop and investigate the text it illustrates. The whole reason for advertising is expensively lost if no one is attracted to read the selling message.

Merchandise shown in an ad is immeasurably easier to draw if the artist has made hundreds or thousands of sketches of items seen anywhere and everywhere. Line drawings of merchandise of many kinds will be requested if the illustrator works for an agency or studio handling retail advertising printed in newspapers, brochures, catalogs and varied mailing pieces.

It's not only important to get the proportions of merchandise correct, but to know how to best show textures of soft goods and hardwares. Some need hard shine, patterns or a fluffy, gentle feel. In many such jobs that I've had, it was left up to the artist to know and choose the best angle from which to view the articles. Sometimes the actual merchandise is brought to the artist for the drawing. The artist will be best equipped for the job if already accustomed to working from "life" rather than copying from pictures.

62 *METHODS*

Lingerie is effectively shown with line treatment. (Courtesy of Mariah Graham.)

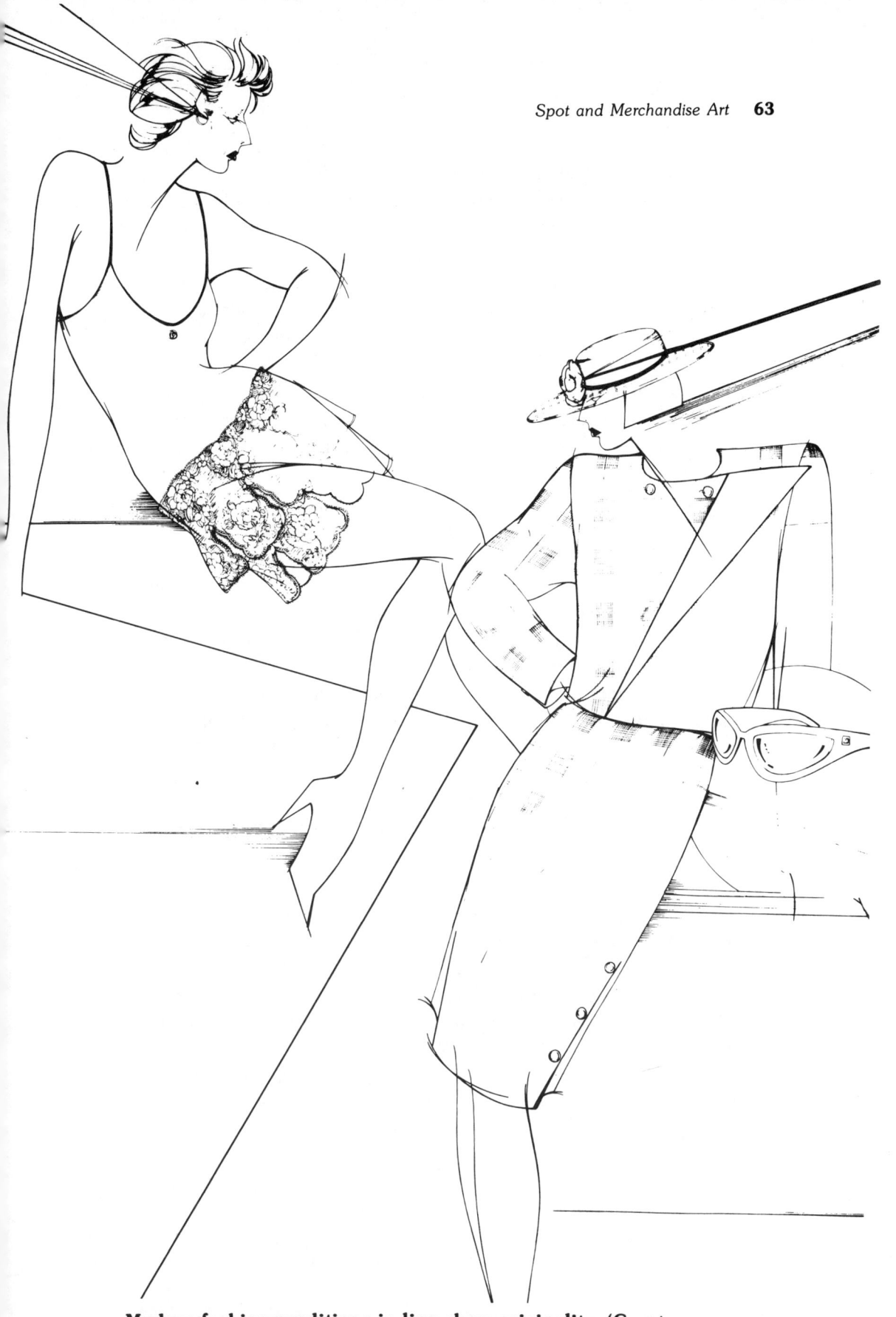

Spot and Merchandise Art 63

Modern fashion renditions in line show originality. (Courtesy of Mariah Graham.)

One large field in merchandise line art, often with tone, is fashion drawing. This isn't intended as a treatise on how-to for fashion drawing, and although a few men have been outstanding as women's fashion artists, the field is largely peopled by women – except for men's clothing. I only wish to point out consideration of fashion as part of a well-rounded ability. It's good to have a diversified portfolio if you wish to keep profitably busy in all seasons as a free-lancer.

Until I was too embroiled in national accounts to have spare time, a fashion account or two was usually a part of my collection of work. The smaller agencies had a diversified clientele and this led to a wide variety of jobs – jewelry, beer, appliances, dishes, bedding and machinery accounts, and political campaigns, to barely touch the kinds encountered.

An important aspect of spot drawings is the ability to create interesting compositions. The art director may only dash in oval shapes to indicate where your art goes. From there it's up to you to compose a grouping of happy people viewing or using the merchandise, maybe only a setting of the products. Tackling such problems is much easier if the artist knows how to arrange elements within a given space.

No matter how small the spot or merchandise drawings will be when printed, they should as a general rule be drawn larger, allowing for some reduction. Most of the time I work size-and-a-half larger. Whenever drawing for reduction, don't forget that line widths also reduce. Allow for this so lines aren't made too thin in the original and thus break up when reduced. Illustrators should all have reducing glasses to see how work will look when smaller. The farther held from the drawing, the greater the reduction.

Since there are many markets for spot drawings, so much merchandise that needs to be shown, and large numbers of art directors who look kindly at spots in an artist's portfolio, then why wouldn't the ambitious illustrator have a few samples of good line art to show? The key word is *good*. Just because spots are usually incidental to the main course – like appetizers – artists shouldn't look down on them as not deserving their best talents and efforts. It would be a good idea to make some spots and merchandise drawings in line and tone. They certainly couldn't hurt your portfolio's effectiveness.

Line figures don't need many details to strikingly serve a purpose. (Reprint permission of Weight Watchers International Inc. © 1986.)

Spot and Merchandise Art   65

Pen and ink illustrations don't need tediously complicated handling to be effective for the needs. (Courtesy University of Redlands, Whitehead Center for Lifelong Learning.)

Solid black with a few needed lines define a subject as complex as an automobile.

66 *METHODS*

There's no limit to the variety of lines you'll need for food.

Practice various line arrangements until you can approximate all kinds of textures in line.

9
Line and Food

A delicious way to approach food is with pen and ink instead of knife and fork. An artist needs only to open the food section of a metropolitan newspaper to see how much line art has nourished the pages. But how do these drawings come about?

No branch of line art uses more varied applications of ink than the myriad textures needed to represent beef, hams, fruits, cakes, vegetables, canned and boxed foods, receptacles from cut crystal to metal – beverage containers, aluminum foil packaging – there's scarcely an end to the artist's imaginative opportunities.

The techniques of food illustration can range from stippling through almost endless ways of laying pen lines, whether parallel and smooth or short little dabs, to coarse dots intermixed with lines, to crosshatching. Obviously, some textures could best be made with tech pens when steady control of fine short lines or dots is desired.

Certainly an essential part of food art is a master-ability to draw accurately. This is not only true with delineating unpackaged items such as meats, fruits, vegetables and baked goods, but is especially demanding when packaged merchandise is to be drawn. It must be accurate as to the proportions of boxes and bottles, and in the lettering of labels. With plastic or glass containers, the food inside might have to be drawn as it would look through that material.

How would you simulate the nubbly skin of an avocado? What to do about a crisp lettuce salad with tomato slices? Can you make

68 METHODS

a cream puff look delicious and different from a baked potato with sour cream topping?

One good way to practice is to raid the refrigerator and cupboards for models. However, keep at the drawings long enough to finish before eating your models! You have many boxes and bottles at home for practice exercises. Develop more than just one way to show the glass – the hardness and shine – the way container material might change the look of food as contrasted to the way it would appear outside on a dish.

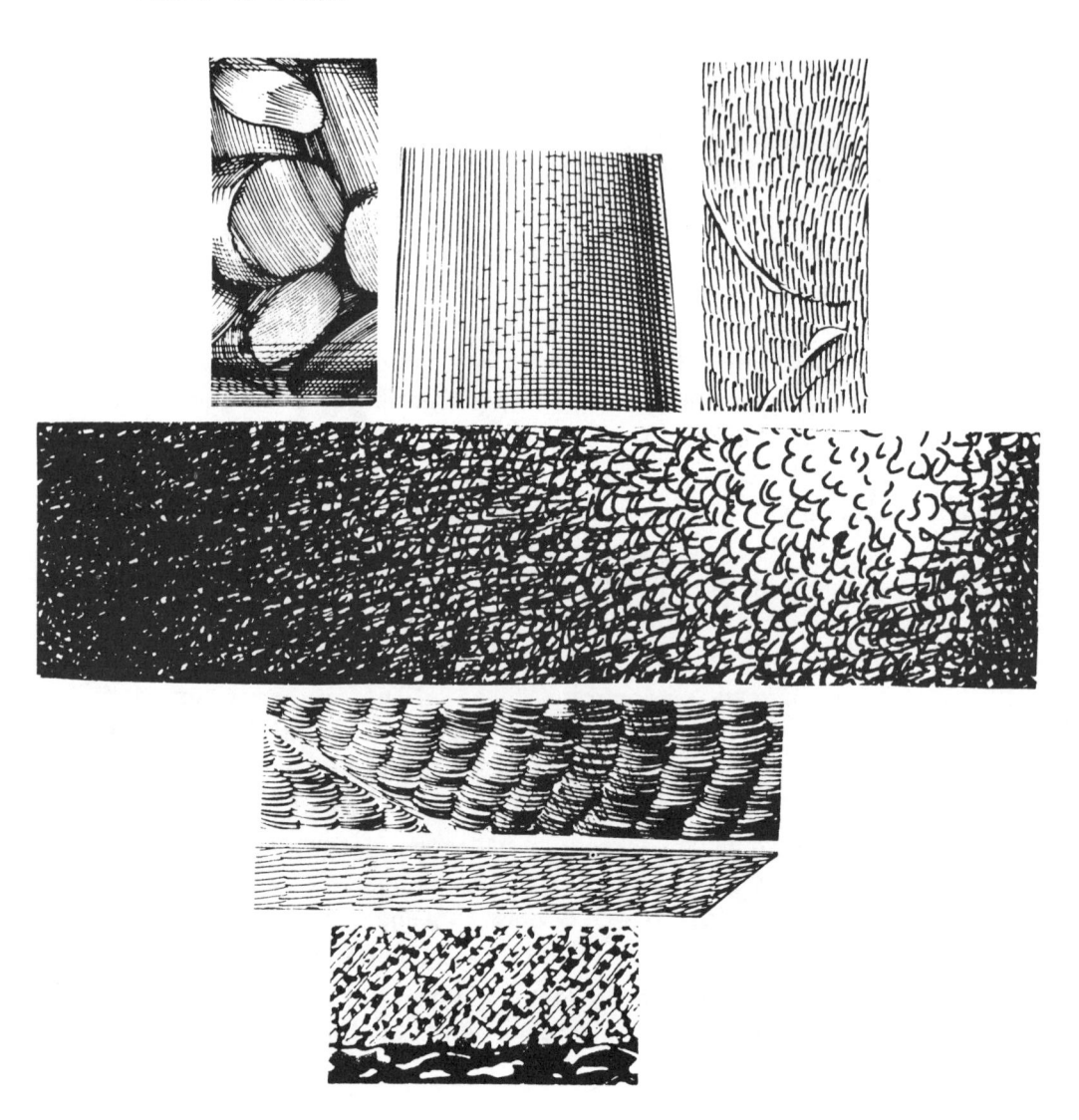

Whether it's meat, cake, avocado, yams or a container, there are textures in line for them.

Study each food to determine which line treatment serves best. Mushrooms have a different treatment than meat or cake.

There's a way with pen and ink to attack any food art problem. With earnest application you may come upon a different and better way to show various textures. Study and practice the many pen and ink textures shown here.

Once you've mastered food art to the point of having what you believe are samples of professional quality showing wide variety, then where should you show them? It's important to not run around futilely to the wrong places. This is where the importance of an *Artist's Market* book becomes apparent.

Advertising agencies with restaurant, food manufacturing, retail food markets, hotels or any other accounts which deal with meals and eating are possible outlets. Some of these businesses, particularly large market chains, have their own advertising departments, usually in their headquarters. Others use ad agency services.

One excellent outlet for food art in line would be clip art services which are listed in the *Artist's Market*. Naturally, it takes time, legwork and questions to learn of food art possibilities around you.

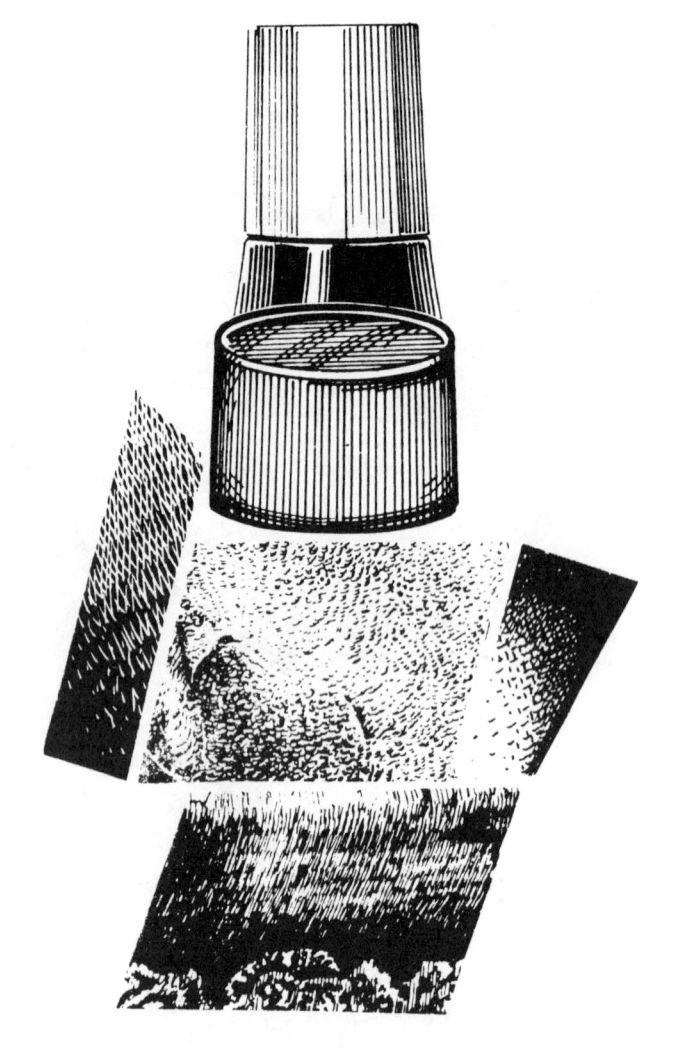

Each kind of line has a place in food illustrating.

A few phone calls could help. Don't forget that some pieces, such as booklets, brochures and catalogs use some form of food art for such appliances as refrigerators, freezers, stoves and the like. Ask dealers for manufacturers' headquarter addresses. Sometimes retailers can tell who does their advertising. Leave no "plate, platter or shelf" uninvestigated to get your resources.

In my ad-art experience I've been called on to make food drawings for local chain bakeries, Norge, Leonard and Kelvinator refrigerators, Heinz foods, gas and electric companies which power stoves, Parke, Davis & Company and even Mercury automobiles. It may be difficult to connect a motorcar with food art, but one ad heading was: "A Recipe for Carefree Driving," which proves an artist can't predict where what request will come from. This is a good argument for preparedness and versatility.

By now you might know whether line art for food is toothsome to you. There are few other branches for black and white line which could give you as much variety of treatment. Examine the pages of newspapers' food supplements. Familiarize yourself with what's being done, bought and used. Food art may prove to be just your "dish."

**Foods, each with totally different lines.
These should be noted
by anyone interested in food line art.**

Loose pen drawings can create dramatic emotional feelings that need no details.

A 2B charcoal pencil sketch done quickly on a camera lucida. The "lucy" helps with spontaneity.

10
Free Lines Wander

Line art needn't be inhibited or stilted because of the narrowness of pen and pencil points or the limitation of black and white. Instead, try the glorious free flourishes which add charm and interest to line drawings as the pen or pencil seemingly wanders. The trick is to work with freedom until you achieve the ultimate aim – a drawing that is technically correct while appearing effortless and spontaneous – even though the intermediate result may give the impression of utter abandon.

How to do this if you've never done it before? Obviously, there aren't hard rules or road maps or shortcuts. The ease of accomplishment arrives only after becoming thoroughly acquainted with the "feel" of the tools in your hand, plus a much practiced friendship with fast sketching – seeing through the clutter to essentials. It took me a considerable time to shed the reticence which couples with the beginning desire to "get it just right." After you've drawn enough, a feeling of assurance creeps in and an essential correctness shines through, allowing the freedom for lines to flourish.

As a practice exercise, take a sheet of fairly smooth paper, a crowquill or #290 Gillott point, then just let the pen wander rather than trying to actually draw any particular subject. Do this until the feel of freedom begins to come.

Loosening is one of the most difficult aspects of drawing to teach. It could be compared to telling a drowning person to let go of a rope which could save his life. One student nodded knowingly enough

Loose freedom with lines. Note how the solid blacks put emphasis where wanted and separates the figures. (By the author for her book, *Guilty of a Skin*.)

when told the pencil sketches showed a fearfulness about being wrong and were strangling the overall effect. What did this person do on the next try? Exactly the same hesitant, niggardly lines which said, "I'm afraid I might be wrong."

Another worrisome idea which interferes with good drawing is that all details *must* be shown. Why? The human eye is a wonderful organ for seeing, then telegraphing to the brain what it sees, even though the objects seen are half-hidden and obscured. Likewise, not every edge or contour need be shown in your drawing. Suggestions are enough. Leave something to the imagination – don't beat the object to death with picky, unnecessary details. Not every leaf on a tree or hair on a head need to be shown.

Again I find myself coming back to the advisability of having much practice with the little sketchbook taken with you everywhere. Your human models aren't going to pose in one position very long, so you're forced to rapidly seek out the essential lines and ignore details.

Drawn in a few minutes with an ordinary ballpoint pen on the cover of a little notebook I carry.

John C. Calhoun drawn with a crowquill pen on vellum. Practice precedes getting the casually sketched look. (Author's illustration for her book, *Guilty of a Skin*.)

A fine crowquill pen on vellum was used. If necessary, work out the direction of toning lines first with pencil. (By the author for her book, *Gone Forever Again*.)

Sometimes great emotions are better-expressed if drawn loosely. A drawing often has a stronger impact when not overladen with unessentials. "Spirit" is gained when the work isn't "overnoodled," as we say in the art business.

If your line drawing is to be a likeness of a certain person, it can still be accomplished without tightening down to a nub for fear of losing the resemblance. The head of John C. Calhoun is an example of letting the features of eyes, brows, nose and mouth carry the look of him. This drawing has lines too fine to withstand reduction.

Getting back to how to get looseness, I can recommend drawing with a camera lucida projection of a photo on your board or paper. This makes it easy to work more loosely, as you can see in the man's head drawn with charcoal pencil. [figure 53] Spontaneity is the name of this method. If you don't own a "lucey," maybe a studio would let you use theirs as long as you don't get in the way when they need it. Several brands of artists' opaque projectors are available, many at modest prices.

Getting back to how to get looseness, I can recommend drawing with a camera lucida projection of a photo on your board or paper. This makes it easy to work more loosely, as you can see in the man's head drawn with charcoal pencil. [figure   ] Spontaneity is the name of this method. If you don't own a "lucey," maybe a studio would let you use theirs as long as you don't get in the way when they need it. Several brands of artists' opaque projectors are available, many at modest prices.

"Smoke dreams" showing an old man's recollections of his youth, demonstrates the fun which can be enjoyed with a fine pen point smoothly gliding over a silky vellum surface. Note especially the various directions tonal lines run, always related to the shapes they tone. Here as in the Calhoun head, the fine lines can't take much reduction.

Another loosening exercise would be to make a quick outline of a subject, no matter whether persons or things, then have ten or twelve clear bond copies made. On these simple outlines you can practice various line treatments as freely and loosely as possible, lightly penciling in the shadow patterns, then inking them as quickly as you can.

After drawing on several copies, take the red-labeled white Liquid Paper intended for copies and see how many lines of your outline copy can be painted out. This practice should bring interesting results. You'll be surprised to discover how many lines can be eliminated because they're unnecessary to the eye's and mind's comprehension of the subject.

No illustrator should think every detail must be included to get across the idea. (Illustration: Gerry Gersten, Agency: Altier & Maynard Com., Client: Hoffman-La Roche, Inc.)

Another proven means is to make the working pencil sketch on tissue – make it quite complete – then put a clean tissue over it and trace down while eliminating some of the detail. Several tissues could be overlaid until you have a true distillation of the essential subject.

Whenever drawing, try to let free lines wander rather than corseting them into rigidly set lines. It's up to you to keep at the exercises and practice drawings until some good day you forget how you once fretted and stewed over every last pore on your subject's nose!

Note the "air" loose pen drawing gives. A tightly-drawn line would not give the movement and emotion as well.

11
Line Portraits

As a prime consideration, portraits should look like distinctive individual people – otherwise they might be more like police department composite representations of suspected criminals. In the eighteenth century Joshua Reynolds said, "A history painter paints man in general; a portrait painter, a particular man, and consequently a defective model." It is not the perfect store window mannequin we look for in a good portrait drawn in line. Such a head will be like a formula set of features which only approximate a human being – not recognizable as an individual.

Charming portrait heads can be drawn in line, and there are many ways to charge them with interest and variety. This is something (thank goodness) that the artist still has over the camera: pens and pencils can lend qualities lacking in the usual slick photo.

The group of heads demonstrates the first point: that each should look like an individual person. Each drawing began from the simplest starting point, a single outline plus lines to indicate the shadow patterns. In all but one of the drawings, these shadow areas have been filled in with parallel lines or crosshatching. The tonal lines were simply drawn freehand, varied with a few solid blacks.

Many more tones may be used on men's heads, but I usually play down brisk techniques on pretty women's faces, preferring to leave mostly white paper except for a slight shadow suggestion. It's difficult to prescribe that pen lines should go this way or that, or how they should be slanted. On some heads shown, lines approximate directions of contours.

80 *METHODS*

These start as simple pen outlines with shadow pattern outlines. Tones can then be easily added.

Franklin D. Roosevelt done with short vertical strokes with a litho pencil. (Author's illustration for her book, *Mama Played Mah-Jongg*.)

Start with simple shadow ideas at first. One suggestion might be to make a single line head outline drawing, then have bond copies made. On these you could block out shadow systems based on different light sources. On some, have all the light come from the right or left side; direct light from one side with a secondary source on the other side. The whole look is changed if top or underlighting is used. They're less usual and more difficult because of less familiar shadow patterns.

82 METHODS

You must lose timidity to put this much pen toning over a face. It's only advisable for men's heads.

Loose line technique looks "dashed off" but is carefully planned for contour directions.

Some outlining of shadow patterns and strong lights from either side. The intent gaze was the main point, details weren't needed.

Line Portraits 85

The versatility of tech pens' techniques is shown in Henry Fonda's portrait in the hands of one well-acquainted with the tool. (Nancy Ohanian, Art Director *Los Angeles Times.*)

General Douglas MacArthur. Until you're used to this loose handling of shadow areas, pencil-in the guidelines first.

If a good bond copier isn't available, you can still do this exercise by laying tissues over your original outline and tracing through, then adding tonal effects. And remember, pens glide well over tracing tissue.

Getting a likeness is easier for some artists than others, but a large amount of the skill has to do with your ability to see correctly, then telegraph to your brain which then directs your hand. It has to do with your ability to know what you see, then translate this knowledge into hand action. The eye has to be a veritable measuring device to judge distances all over the head and face, otherwise features will be drawn with ears too high or low.

General MacArthur's head is more complicated, but notice that again shadow areas are lightly outlined. The light hit many areas of his characterful face. The cap and clothes add considerable complication.

I had a fine portrait teacher who gave unforgettable suggestions. For instance, isn't it true that we can recognize people we know even when they're so far away that details can't be seen? How do we know who they are? By the shapes of shadow patterns such as eye socket areas, hair shape, body size and carriage. It's a whole study of what makes this person different from others.

You must plan ahead to locate where solid blacks will soften out on edges, and where the pure paper highlights will be. (By author for her book, *Guilty of a Skin*.)

This pen line treatment is good for older men's heads.

Even if you don't have much call for portraits of actual people, you may do heads and figures for ads or editorial material. These are what I classify as the "happy beautiful people" who're always smiling or looking pleasantly at the product or merchandise, from the diamond ring on her finger to the car he's about to buy. Unlike actual portraits, these men and women are usually closer to the "ideal," with uncomplicated shadow tones. They're generally handled more lightly because they could be compared to extras in the movies – necessary adjuncts, but subordinate to the stars which are the advertised products. Being able to draw well is the prerequisite for this type of line art because there usually aren't models from which to draw. You must bring the beautiful people from your storehouse of ability, memory, or your idea file.

If you decide to pursue free-lance accounts, then own an up-to-date *Artist's Market*. It's filled with information about hundreds of art markets. It's the "bible" for artists who wish to track down all possibilities.

Should you wish to specialize with portrait heads, you must determine which magazines use occasional heads of (usually) well-known people. Those which seem the likeliest could be sent bond copies of your best heads.

If you live in a city with galleries, you should contact them, showing original portraits nicely matted or framed. They might be a source for commissions. Contact newspapers in your area for their possible need of line heads. Contact every possible buyer, even making line heads of friends and family for samples. Many artists have managed successful, happy careers by making line portraits. The key to these attainments lay with the ability of the artist, both in art and salesmanship.

The charm of the model's expression caught with black Berol Prismacolor pencil #935 on lightly-toothed paper. (Courtesy David Smiton, artist, Hartsdale New York, *Artist's Market* 1986)

90 METHODS

Mixed mediums, pastel, marker and charcoal, were used for this imaginative fashion illustration. (Artist: Jacques Alscheck for PROPHECY Corp., Carrollton, Texas.)

12
Combining Line With Tone

Adding tone to line art by any of several means is often desired by art directors or advertisers because of the extra dimension it can give simplified line drawings. The variety of effects is almost endless, from the many mediums for toning to the way these materials can be handled.

It's advisable to include examples of line art with tone in your portfolio to show the spread of work you can handle. On an actual job the art director will likely indicate whether you should add tone. Reproduction will require a halftone shot of the wash combined with a line shot of the pen lines. This will cost more to produce. These production steps – and costs – are points you must consider when splashing on tone or color. Pure line cuts are the cheapest way out for the client.

Transparent wash can be applied in several ways, either placed in specific areas as a flat tone, or smooth except for brushed-out edges. The ink drawing must be done with waterproof ink and allowed to dry thoroughly before applying the wash.

If you aren't familiar with Bourges sheets, you should become acquainted with this highly useful addition to line art. They are acetate sheets which come in a wide range of colors. The entire drawing can be covered or smaller pieces cut and taped to the art if only small areas of the tone are needed.

The surface on the duller side can be scratched away with a plastic stylus where not wanted. For some effects I've found that scratching

The tonal effect over and around the flowers could be a transparent wash or a graduated-dot mechanical screen with the few whites scratched out. (Courtesy Norm Bendell, represented by David Goldman Agency.)

with various grades of steel wool will leave interesting edges. The control and use of the wool can only be gained by experimentation on practice pieces of Bourges.

Another valuable material for line art is the "Ben Day" screen (named after its inventor, an American printer). Actually, there are hundreds of varieties, sold under brand names such as Zipatone, Letratone, and Formatt. Each screen consists of a pattern of dots printed on self-adhesive acetate. The acetate film is affixed directly to the line drawing by burnishing gently. Then a thin-bladed frisket knife is used to cut the desired areas of the screen, and the parts not wanted are pulled away. Optically, the dot pattern appears as a particular shade of grey, creating a combination line/halftone drawing without adding to production costs.

Craftint is another invaluable method to quickly and cheaply get halftone effects in a drawing which can be reproduced with a single line shot. Craftint paper already contains the pattern undeveloped. Two-tone Craftint requires two bottles of developer. With the ink drawing already on the Craftint paper, the first developer is brushed on and a pattern of a parallel lines appears. When this has dried, the other developer is brushed where a darker tone is wanted, making visible a second set of parallel lines crosshatching the lighter tint to double the value of tone.

To be successful with double-tone Craftint, a separate brush should be used for each developer so the chemicals aren't intermixed or diluted by a brush that's been in water. I must admit it takes time to become accustomed to the smell of the dark-tone developer. Don't bend your nose too close to the bottle.

After developing both tones, you can go back with pen and ink to cross edges with fine lines at a different angle. This gives a graduated edge more nearly like halftone gradations. The same changing of edges may be done by crossing the Craftint lines with a fine brush of opaque white. The finished product may be economically shot as a line drawing.

While cost considerations are more crucial in retail ads than national, you have several options for getting maximum effectiveness while minimizing production costs. Adding tone to your line drawings should put a gleam in the client's eye. Include some of these among your samples.

The toning on this litho pencil line drawing of Hitler, would have a halftone screen when reproduced. (Book illustration for author's *Johnny Went Marching Out*.)

94 METHODS

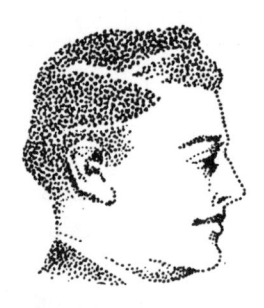

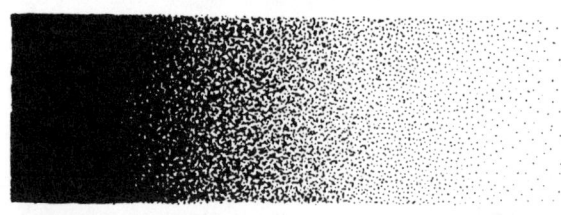

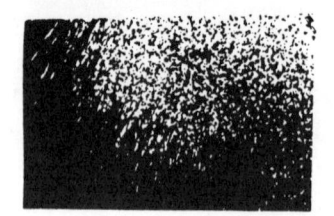

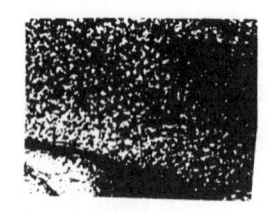

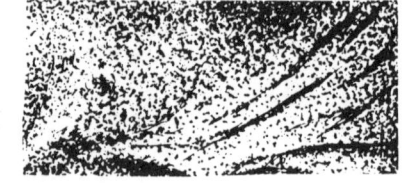

Stippling practice swatches.

Stippling masterfully executed while Mr. Raccoon posed. (Courtesy Ken Hull, Boalsburg, State College, PA)

13
Stippling Returns

Reappearance of stippling as a pen-and-ink treatment reminds me of the old saying about fashion, "If you wait long enough, styles will come back in style." Stippling is somewhat like pointillism, the Neo-Impressionist painting method which consisted of unblended points or spots of paint.

What has caused a resurgence in patiently making tiny ink dots to form tones and gradations in black-and-white drawings? The technical pen long favored by engineering draughtsmen. Its tiny, tubular nib can make perfect dots. A popular brand is the Koh-I-Noor Rapidograph, with a refillable ink cartridge and thirteen nibs which make different line widths. Other brands are: Mars, Rotring (also made by Koh-I-Noor) and Faber Castell TG. The tubular nib works smoothly in all directions on any smooth Bristol or Strathmore boards or papers, hot-pressed illustration board and even (with special ink) on such slick surfaces as acetate.

For those who contemplate putting some stipple samples in their portfolios, I'd like to suggest that as far as advertising art is concerned, stipple drawings aren't prevalently used. It's a limited market commercially. The first and most obvious reason is the time needed to complete an involved subject in a business famous for its rush rush deadlines.

Another problem is making changes or corrections in stippled art without scars showing. The best of artists are often asked to make changes – it's a normal part of the game. This is a good argument for using a high quality surface that can withstand the punishment of erasures and still retain a usuable surface.

Stippling lends itself to food art in various ways.

I checked with art directors in fifteen states about the market for stipple art as they see it. Nine of them said either an outright no or that it's a limited market. They feel that this art doesn't reduce well, which curtails its use since much ad-art is used in several sizes; it's tedious and time-consuming to create, thus limiting it to only special jobs.

On the positive side, since other directors had affirmative replies, the uncertainty is resolved – you *should* include a sample or two to demonstrate your ability in this technique.

Don't despair about efforts you've expended in this direction, because there are outlets for fine work. It's good for newspapers as long as it isn't greatly reduced. It can also work well for book illustration; as commissions to produce portraits, exhibition pieces for galleries and clip art firms. There's no better way to create an awareness of your patient ability than to have your work shown as much as possible so many will see it. This means entering shows and being accepted by good galleries.

Guilty of a Skin

Stippling provided a striking graphic treatment for the head on this book cover design.

Specialization of subject matter is a good accompaniment to your specific technique. One artist has a wide market for her stippling because she chiefly does impressive fish pictures which are popular with the multitudes of fishermen. Another artist makes eye-catching portraits of American Indians. In fact, although we usually think of portraits as full-color painted or pastel works, the stipple method produces arresting results. One man specializes in old home pictures and historical covered bridges while another does landscapes. Greeting card companies could use stippled drawings. Some artists have done chiefly architectural themes or western and wildlife subjects. One lady has an unusual branch – aviation illustrations. Possibilities are endless.

How do most artists proceed with this technique? Naturally, each artist develops a personalized approach to stippling even though many agree on the type of pen and paper which works for best results. Nearly all prefer to work from photos so the images "sit still" while they work all of the hours to complete a picture. Some make their own camera shots. Most also make careful pencil under-drawings before an ink dot is placed, so they know exactly where they're going. It could be disastrous after perhaps much work, to find one's dots had wandered astray enough to distort the subject or background.

The time expended by some stipplers can run many hours, possibly into days or weeks. Unless time is of no concern to the artist, it's imperative to carefully plan the basic drawing, indicating where what tones will go. Later the pencil guides can be erased.

To determine the various intermediates between full black and white, it's useful to have a scale of graduated greys as a tonal guide. Do stippling exercises until a smooth transition in tones comes easily.

There are variations as to artist preferences in renditions. Some go from the darkest darks to lightest light (pure paper), whereas others are more in control if they go from lightest to dark. I've always liked best to get the solid blacks placed, then key subsequent tones down from there. In nib sizes, some prefer 0000 to 2, but one expert in the technique never uses a nib larger than 000. Then another swears by 000 to 4. To keep successfully dotting away, no matter what point size you prefer, tech pens need tender loving care and cleaning.

Out there are some receptive art directors. The more you work at this technique, the faster and easier it will develop.

With a fine point and patience, whether with tech pen or stiff fine conventional art pen point, animals may be done by building short lines, stipples, and solids. (Courtesy Maupintour, Inc.)

Silhouettes combined with dotted outlines form eye-catching shapes and contrasts. (Courtesy Grove Homes, Rancho Carlsbad.)

Don't overlook what a brush with ink can do. The blacks add solidity to the piece.

Compelling simplicity of composition weds a large furniture outlet with the Tacoma Grand Prix logo. (Courtesy Schoenfeld's Furniture, Tacoma, Washington. Tacoma Grand Prix Assoc. for logo.)

III / THE BUSINESS OF LINE ART

14
What Art Directors Buy

In the working advertising artist's life there's no person who has more say over whether he or she is in or out on a job than the art or creative director. This isn't forgetting the client or others who express likes or dislikes when they see drawings, but the artist rarely comes in direct contact with these people if working for a studio or agency. The director is "Mr. or Ms. Big" in the artist's dealings with buyers of illustration. Since it's important to know what they say about line art and black-and-white illustrations, I surveyed a number of art directors around the country.

Because it's necessary to know there's a ready market for what you have to sell, the first question I asked art and creative directors was, "Is there presently a constant market for pen and ink illustrations and line spots?" Overwhelmingly art directors agreed that line spots in many techniques are in constant demand. Only a few agencies had little call for line art, due to the nature of their accounts.

To avoid false expectations about the position the work will have in an advertisement, the next logical question was, "Are these illustrations subordinate parts of layouts or the key art of an ad?" Slightly over half said that this type of artwork is subordinate to the main illustration, photo or text.

The majority of other directors said they have used line art for both key and subordinate spots. Two said they always use line drawings as key art, probably due to the type of accounts they have. The others described the drawings' use as depending on the product and projects' overall needs and design. Clearly, line art isn't necessarily relegated to a position of minor importance.

I was curious about the directors' attitudes toward possible markets for black-and-white drawings rendered in such mediums as charcoal, Wolff pencil, litho pencil and pastel used as line. It was almost surprising to hear the amount of positive responses to this question since these mediums are generally used for their ability to render grey tones, while good reproduction in line requires crisp blacks.

Most commentators said, "Yes, unreservedly," that they were receptive to these mediums. Three as positively replied, "No," but many said there is a minimal market, depending on the ability of the artist to prepare art so it reproduces well in line. Otherwise, if the work needs to be reproduced as a halftone, the purpose of line art is lost. One director said it would only be used as editorial art – probably political or other cartoons. Three specified that style and expert handling were the determining factors.

If your portfolio includes a sample or two drawn excellently in any of these mediums, crispness of handling will have to be uppermost to command a favorable reception.

I next asked, "Is the technical pen prevalent in today's line art?" The answer was an avalanche of yeses. Only one agency indicated limited use of it, another seemed unfamiliar with the implement, while others praised technical pens as the greatest innovation since windshield wipers.

Considering the overwhelming acceptance of this tool, it behooves the aspiring artist to invest in a technical pen – unless lucky enough to have one furnished by the agency or studio. With practice and earnest application, it should be money well-spent which can guarantee good returns.

The artist who wishes to stay abreast of what's happening should prepare for the influx of computer graphics. More and more hi-tech advances are invading even the ad-art field whether we like it or not.

What Art Directors Buy **103**

NANCY OHANIAN / for The Times

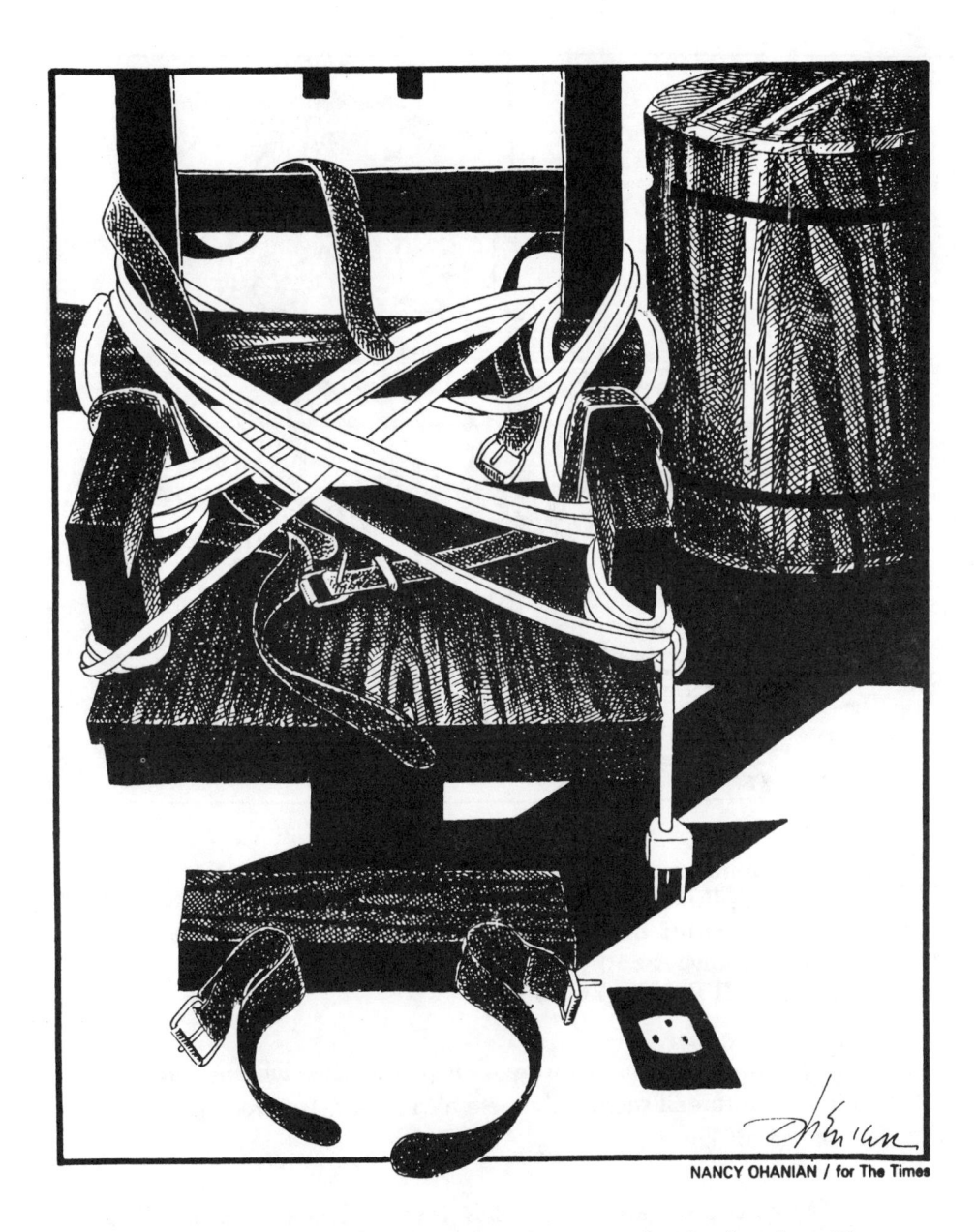

For objects or portraits, this artist has an individual style with the KOH-I-Noor Rapidograph pen. (Courtesy Nancy Ohanian, Art Director *Los Angeles Times.***)**

Where cameras may not go, artists are needed to sketch courtroom proceedings. They must draw quickly and get likenesses. This line art could be perfected by much previous work in the sketch pad, always with you, that's been recommended. (Courtesy Bill Robles, KCBS-TV.)

Art directors are becoming aware of its possibilities, whether now or in the near future. It seems advisable also for artists to recognize this fact of the art life.

"When you see artists' portfolios, is much line art shown?" The answer to this question could tell job-seeking artists whether they'd have steady competition in line drawings; whether art directors were eager to see more or didn't really care if it was in the showings. Any help in knowing what to present should be welcome.

One art director lamented that not enough line art comes to his desk, while six said they see no line art in portfolios. This could mean several things: would-be artists haven't been taught the importance of a balanced portfolio, aren't aware of the amount of line art bought, or they prefer to dabble with pretty colors. They may look on line art as a "lesser" art form, not worthy of their time.

One director said not enough basic drawing is taught in schools, while those who see some line art remarked that much of it isn't especially good. Two agencies reported line drawings as 30% and 50% of the art they see. "Minimal amount" was one reply. According to one art director: "I only see line from specialized illustrators, as most young artists come out of art schools with a desire to show their colorful pieces."

Single lines give full tonality when run in various combinations. (Courtesy The Camera Shop, Tacoma, Washington.)

Looking through the answers, plus all the years of my experience as a staffer and free-lance, I can highly recommend having a healthy showing of the best line art of which you're capable. It's much more likely to sell for you than the brightest, most complicated full-color illustration you ever made – at least in your beginning stabs at the business.

"Wouldn't you encourage young artists to keep line art high on their list of skills?"

A solid majority of directors agreed that job-seeking artists should polish their line art samples, then carry their *best* pieces in portfolios. One enlarged the answer by saying, "Line art teaches precision and cleanliness of presentation." (Let's hope so!)

Several said more than a simple "yes" on the subject. A Nebraska agency art director says he sees more line art in younger artists' showings. He adds, "I do a lot of small line spots because I enjoy illustrating in my own style."

Montage assemblies of various places or things are particularly suitable for travel advertising. The solids help it to read well. (Courtesy Provident Federal Savings.)

Imagination and inventiveness are necessary for pen and ink success. (Courtesy Nancy Ohanian, Art Director *Los Angeles Times*.)

In California, one gave a provocative answer by starting with a blunt "no." But he continued knowingly, "I would point out the importance of it. Every young artist is aiming for full-color illustrations. Until they get over that stage and experience, time will teach them the importance of line art." To which I can only add "Amen."

Art directors in New Mexico and Massachusetts agencies gave resounding affirmatives. The former –"Yes! If you can't draw, you can't present your ideas to clients." Further, this agency especially looks for the ability to draw clean precise art, realistic pen and ink illustrations. The eastern director enthusiastically stated, "You bet – yes – it's the main craft!"

Some buyers suggested flexibility and diversification in the collection of work to tote when job-hunting.

"This is a tedious, exacting method requiring ultimate patience, great drawing skills and much time. I'm sure some agencies would use illustrations done in this method." What is the method mentioned by a New Jersey agency art director? It's stippling. I've been seeing so much black-and-white art with this technique lately, it seemed wise to ask the art directors, "Is there a market for present stippling as done with tech pens?"

The variety of what can be done with line styles is almost endless. (Courtesy Parke-Davis, Div. Warner Lambert Co.)

Nearly all of them I quizzed resoundingly said yes to the tech pen stipple style in black-and-white art. For more about stippling, see the chapter, "Stippling Returns."

The art directors also offered many other excellent comments and recommendations, such as: "Line art works great in newspapers — use bolder lines for better reproduction." (Especially if art is to be reduced.)

Excellent advice from a New Jersey art director: "Basically the work must be clean and neat — no smudges or fingerprints. After all, a messy portfolio cannot represent clean work. I suggest artists do not include anything they must apologize for — I put this in because — although I do like to see a rough and comp layout to the finished piece. Not necessarily a photostat, but a good clean machine copy is usually sufficient for me to get an idea of the artist's ability to handle my type of work."

More sage advice from Des Moines, Iowa: "Show a wide range of subject matter done well, or limited subject matter done superbly — both if able."

More good hints: "When showing a portfolio which includes line art, try to show a variety of styles and subject matter — people, nature, hard goods. They should include line, stipple, crosshatching and such.

Another great example is to enlarge artwork twice up and reduce the same twice down from the original."

Another wisely suggested, "Many artists require knowledge of newspaper printing so the piece they create will get the maximum quality. So much black-and-white art becomes washed out on newspaper stock – even on the paper used by *The Wall Street Journal*."

More solid counsel: *"Don't forget the basics!* One might have a great technique or style, but if it's laid down on an illustration that doesn't show a knowledge of body, skeleton form, perspective, lighting, et cetera, it's not usable or worth the effort. A good loose, understandable style is not often seen today."

Any ad-art hopeful should stand at attention and heed such words as these: "The ability to draw is the single most valuable skill to an artist in advertising today. The skill of communicating with drawings in a clear, accurate and creative way, coupled with linguistic proficiency allows an ad person to choose his position." (This last should be an invigorating thought for ambitious young artists.)

Good advice poured in, not only for the benefit of line artists, but for anyone pounding on the ad-art doors for work. "Only include your best pieces and only those that would reproduce well. Develop a 'style' or 'look' to your work. This will often influence the designer who wants to create a certain look for an ad. It helps if the illustrator is versatile as well."

One large agency buys only line art of automotive or mechanical subjects. It's important in such instances – if not all – to learn what accounts are carried so the erring artist doesn't present drawings of ladies' lingerie where machinery parts would be more appropriate. A call or letter can help to avoid such situations.

One director's single-word comment was "realism." In ad-art there's still a market for drawings but they should have class and style as well as accuracy. Another briefly said, "Develop a style of your own."

"Being an artist is a profession, and like other professions it is a constant matter of improving one's skills. Much like actors, the more your work is seen, the more in demand you will be." Up until now we haven't much discussed exposure, but no matter how fine your drawings, they'll do little for you in a drawer. Another art director adds what could be a postscript to the foregoing, "Keep on trying." Persistence works wonders.

Each line artist can evolve into an individual "style" without realizing when it happens. (Illustration: Gerry Gersten, Agency: Altier & Maynard, Client: Hoffman-LaRoche, Inc.)

Although artists should always strive for quality, one art director touched another facet: "Be aware of the client's product. Assign yourself jobs." (Such as constantly making fresh samples to show.) "Talk's cheap because this is a 'show-me' business." Telling art directors what you can do doesn't cut it in job-seeking.

These comments from a cross section of art and creative directors in many states should give you an idea of what they're looking for. If the samples you're peddling seem a bit tired and worn, or have received criticism in some places, then it's time to retire them while you dig into making some sparkling bright new "salesmen" for your portfolio.

A Texas art director spelled out in a few words the very essence of what's needed in today's market. "Be heavily commercial and technically brilliant (or get into another line of work)!" We must never get so "arty" that we forget we're primarily in a commercial business, and the demands for excellence never cease.

We're all understandably interested in money for work done. Line artists are no different (and shouldn't be), considering the amount of time and exertion necessary to make saleable line art. But how much should you charge, and how much will the buyer pay?

"In pricing," said one art director, "try to put an hourly value on your artwork. Then base it on experience plus the usage of the piece. This should give all concerned a fair price." Another said, "The market values artwork based upon the skills exhibited and current needs."

More detailed remarks: "Until an artist can develop a demand for his or her work, pricing should be a matter of selling commensurate with what the client will pay. I believe artists can do better by representing themselves rather than selling through an agent." (Unless you can spare his percentage off your price.)

Quality of work was repeatedly stressed when it comes to pricing. It stands to reason that line art can't command as high a rate as full-color paintings, but an accomplished black-and-white line artist can have an acceptable income if the work is good and in demand.

A well-known expression in studio pricings is "What the market will bear." Nevertheless one art director said, "Keep pricing directed to a market budget, don't price at 'what the market will bear.' Establish a fair, honest price of what your work is worth and go with it."

Speaking from the agency-client standpoint, another art director says, "Naturally we all want the best possible for the least cost. The artist must determine the value of his own time and art. If he/she is in great demand, naturally the rate will be higher than for a person just beginning. The amount of detail required, size of the finished piece and time involved in achieving the client's requirements should all be taken into consideration when pricing a job."

Two directors spelled out actual figures: "Keep it at $35 per hour maximum," and "$300 to $500 per work day." You should expect, however, to find many variations in prices on both sides of these figures. For specific help in pricing, The *Graphic Artists Guild Handbook* is a useful guide.

In may own art experience with many types of markets, agencies and studios, I must say there were many differences in pricing practices. We *did* sometimes go by "what the market will bear" and it was sweet! With time and experience the problem should become resolved and less of a quandary. Happy earning to you!

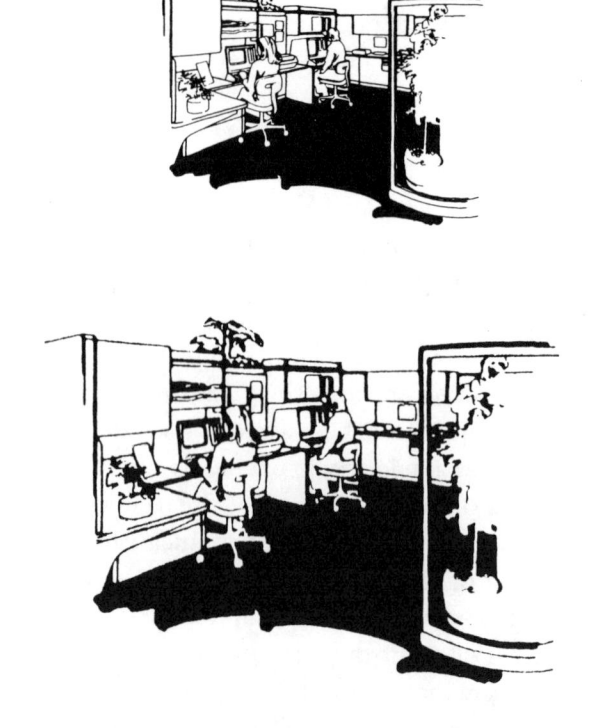

If a line illustration is to be reduced, allow for the fact that line widths also reduce. (Courtesy The Stationers, Inc., Tacoma, Washington.)

15

An Artist's Line Experience

At best the art market is mercurial, and it's imperative for artists to stay flexible, attentive to new trends in the marketplace. It's all right to specialize and develop your distinctive style – your "trademark"– so long as you don't close the shutters to change and new challenges.

During my years in illustration, I had to learn, unlearn and adopt new techniques numbers of times. Just as I was proud of being able to draw flawlessly smooth pen lines in any direction, suddenly an art director called for loose lines which I'd never used before. It took a good bit of practice to quickly switch. I've had to learn to keep abreast regardless of how one type of pen line had been perfected.

An artist with whom I once worked had an attitude which could easily do in an artist who doesn't care about eating regularly. He considered his "style" strictly his own mark of distinction and he told the contact man who was trying to sell his work, "Either they buy my illustrations the way they are – or they don't buy them. It's my name they're buying." They never heard of his "name," so they didn't buy. Ego was sorely getting in the way of this fellow's success. (He didn't work there long.)

If you choose to free-lance, the breadth of your stable of customers is directly dependent on the effort you put out to keep accounts and gain new ones. You need to be as much of a business person as an artist. Since art for advertising *is* a business as much as any other, all of your time can't be at the drawing board unless you can afford to have another qualified person handle the contact and mundane business matters. Having this help can cut into your profits.

For the moment let's consider you've decided to try selling cartoons to magazines – this is a good choice because so many use cartoons now. How do you approach them with your funny material? First you thoroughly acquaint yourself with the sort of cartoons each magazine is using. One suitable for *Good Housekeeping* probably wouldn't be bought by *Playboy*.

Don't just submit one batch of cartoons then fold up in a snit if that group isn't bought or even one taken from five or six sent. Consider any of several reasons why they might have been passed over – they didn't strike anyone's funnybone sufficiently, they weren't well enough drawn or distinctive, the subjects weren't appropriate for the selected publication.

Once you've decided on a particular market, keep sending batch after batch of whatever type of art you produce (Providing, of course, that it's of saleable quality) and your name will eventually become familiar. Without this stubborn streak and ability to keep at it, you're quickly self-defeated.

Line art cartoons, possibly combined with tonal effects, should each be tailored for the publication you have in mind. *Know your market* before trying to sell to it! Study more than one issue until you see their style and general content. As often as this point has been harped on by art directors and editors, artists still submit drawings willy-nilly because they and Aunt Minerva admire the work. Sad to say, this doesn't guarantee a sale.

Another plus for entering the cartoon market is because this art can flow in a stream to publications, unsolicited, while illustrations or other work is usually only given by assignment. The cartoon market is wide open. If you're new to this, don't forget that it's much more difficult to "start at the top." Smaller, lower-paying publications are easier to crack if you really wish to get into print.

Will your work reproduce well? Some artists neglect this working knowledge, leaving such detail to some invisible person "over there." But the published result will be only as good as your ability to prepare art which will reproduce well. Where cartooning is concerned,

Free understated lines with a #290 Gillott pen point. The tone was transparent wash laid on a damp strip on hot press illustration board.

A flexible pen made the basic ink drawing and a charcoal pencil added the toning. (Book illustration by the author for her book, *Film City and Suburbs*.)

some young artists think such drawings don't have to be as carefully done as "serious" illustrations. Nothing could be further from the truth, however, because a thorough knowledge of how to draw people and things should underlie all such efforts.

Establishing an aura of reliability to deliver *what* is wanted *when* it's wanted, once you have the job in hand, is the shortcut to an art director's or editor's heart. These important people in an artist's life like to feel secure instead of being hung on a limb as deadline dates approach. This isn't too much to ask of an artist.

An artist can't afford to be too sensitive to criticism if wishing to "make it" in line drawings or any other medium used in advertising art. Certainly it hurts to stand beside an art director's desk while your brain-child is verbally shredded. But you should consider it as free schooling from an expert even though you may not agree at the moment. If you're *not* new to the business, then you'd better take stock, listen better to instructions and sharpen your skills.

If you're free-lancing by mail, then consider it a blessing if the busy art director (I've never seen many unbusy ones) takes time to give criticism or suggestions when replying. The AD must have been somewhat interested to take time to "talk" to you, however briefly. If you strike such chords consistently, it's an almost sure thing that you're on the right road and it's only a matter of time until your destination looms ahead. Remember, the sky's the limit and outer space isn't crowded with artists.

Art instruction is fine but it can be a curse if it's too narrowly directed – demanding that drawings only be done this way or that, on certain paper of specific dimensions and surface. The artists whose work we enjoy and remember, the ones dubbed *successful*, are innovators. It would serve a broader purpose to tell an artist to learn to look at – really study – the subject, rather than to say what kind of lines to make.

A little should be said about *technique* since so many young artists are technique-conscious. They spend too much time trying to gain a special style, a so-called trademark that says who did it, that they may stint on more important points.

Individual style can't be dug out by sheer dint of concentration. Instead, style or technique should come – will come – naturally as a product of seeing the subject thoroughly and having the resulting drawing evolve from your individual way of seeing, then directing your hand to do what you've learned through practice. Your drawing technique will be as personalized as your written signature. It's the true professional who knows the power of a few well-chosen lines to tell about the subject without elaboration or straining for effects.

There are parallels between writing and art. One of the most noticeable is *theme*, but it's not always easily understood in the beginning. As in writing, it demands to be at the bottom of all art or there's nothing but empty purpose. Whether the work is done seriously or humorously, what does it say about the human condition? This is theme, and it's particularly necessary in cartooning.

Certainly art, whether a full-color painting on a gallery wall or line drawing for advertising, reflects something of the human state at the time it's made. I vividly recall the drabness of much art in the worst years of the "Great Depression" when the dull work reflected the mood of the people, the economic hopelessness. It was like a barometer of the times. Some dubbed such art and its producers the "Cult of the Ugly" or "Mud Cult."

When you wish to turn line drawing into dollars, remember the idea's the thing. This is especially true when you set out to dazzle an art director with samples to get free-lance jobs. If you're approaching agencies and studios, learn what sorts of accounts they handle, then gear your samples as much as possible in those directions. It's the old story that people readily respond to and identify with things they know. It makes art directors click to attention if they have accounts for designer label furnishings and that's the subject of your samples. Farm tractors, no matter how well drawn and rendered, would fail to arouse such interest.

Without a good idea, drawing can become no more than a lot of time put in on a hobby. And it will pay about the same. Old ideas are forever waiting for the clever artist who can give them a fresh treatment. Tired subjects can be immeasurably freshened with new twists. After all, there are only so many potential situations, but the differ-

An Artist's Line Experiences 119

Litho pencil portrait of Joseph Stalin. Each stroke is made separately and the main focus is on the eyes. (Book illustration by the author for her book, *Mama Played Mah-Jongg*.)

ence in successful artists and just so-so ones are their abilities to breathe new life into these subjects.

There are no formulas or road maps for how to achieve fresh insights because these have to develop in the creative brain of the artist. Otherwise, we could ask our friendly garage mechanic. He may know all about cars, but it's the job of an artist to come up with a selling, eye-catching drawing on paper.

Artists have the same chances to express creative ideas with their line drawings as writers with their deft use of words. Sometimes the drawings may look deceptively simple, but that is usually harder to do than a cluttered piece. The accomplished artist sees down through to the essential parts, character, trait or action without belaboring the process en route. Surely this is the essence of a cartoonist's job, as well as the line illustrator's or designer's.

Drawn with HB and 2B Wolff pencils.

Although it's great to travel – "broadening" as they say, informative and fun – it takes time and lots of money. But you may get ideas for line drawings as close as your proverbial backyard or the back of your brain. If you are free-lance, this condition always exists; where are the jobs, how am I going to get them all finished, where is the money, if busy making money then where is the time? This might account for some artists doing extended traveling after retiring unless they're lucky enough to have assignments which send them to interesting places. I've known several who've had this good fortune in their free-lance lives. Expenses paid for them, of course.

From an economic standpoint, think how much cheaper it is for artists to tote sketch pads wherever they go than to bear the cost of photo-taking. Of course, there are some problems that call for photographic information, and here it might be better to photograph than sketch, as I learned on one painful occasion. An artist should be able to operate a good camera.

I had traveled out to the coke plant of the Ford Motor Company and selected the most dramatic angle from which to show it. I parked on a small nearby street after being sure there wasn't a no parking sign. I settled with a large bond layout pad propped against the steering wheel and dove into a pencil line sketch. All went smoothly until a tap came on the window.

I looked out at a mountainous policeman bending to look in on what I was doing. Concentrating on the drawing, I hadn't heard his approach. He didn't look like the friendly cop on the beat, and almost immediately there were three squad cars parked behind me. "What are you doing?" he asked.

"Doesn't it look as if I'm sketching?" I was irritated by the interruption. "Am I parked illegally?"

"No, but why are you doing this?" He wouldn't give up.

"I have an assignment to draw an industrial plant and this one looked best for my purpose."

"Who do you work for? What's the phone number?"

Suddenly it came to me why I was of interest to these officers – it was during the Korean War and they'd pegged me as an insidious spy! I offered the sketch to him, but he declined. Finally I asked, "Isn't it true that I could slowly roll along here and take several photos of the plant and you'd never know it?"

Crisp simplicity with a charcoal pencil. Less facial tone usually enhances a woman's portrait.

"W-why yes, I guess so."
"Then that's just what I'll do!"

This anecdote should illustrate the necessity of care about where and when to sketch or take pictures, especially if you should be in an Iron Curtain airport.

Line drawings might be considered inferior to large full-color painted illustrations, both in the amount of payment and in the feeling of importance the more involved work can give. However, it's almost as ego-tickling to have a steady flow of work in the field of line drawing.

Fine crowquill pen lines form full tonality. Solid black area behind the head emphasizes the side light.

Once you've gained skill with handling pens and pencils as a quick way to have a saleable commodity, you'll be able to lessen the idle gaps in free-lancing and will also be more hirable as a staff artist. It's better to be steadily able to sell your black-and-white work than to get the fancier requests only now and then.

Another consoling thought is that a real love can develop for the clean, crisp look of well-executed line drawings. I say this from my years in the business, the steadiness of my income and the many outlets for what was produced. I hope the foregoing thoughts from my experiences will give aid and comfort to those now embarking on line art, whether as a full career or an accompaniment with other types of ad-art. You'll find that broad experience and flexibility can make the market much less mercurial.

Acknowledgments

Grateful appreciation to those who contributed to the pictorial and opinion portions about line art.

Erin Ries, Art Director, Image Dynamics, Inc.
Anne Esposite, Art Director, Duke Unlimited, Inc.
Tobia L. Meyers, Art Director, Morvay Advertising Agcy., Inc.
Robert McAndrew, Art & Creative Director, McAndrew Advertising
Max Rauer, Art Director, LaGrave Klipfel, Inc.
Robert G. Washburn, Vice-Pres/Creative Dir. Creative House
  Adv., Inc.
Alvin Joe, Art Director, Wank, Willimas & Neylan
Patrick S. Osborne, Sr. Art Director, Miller, Friendt Ludemann, Inc.
Joe McDonnell, Art Director, Airy Advertising, Inc.
Bill Reynolds, Art Director, Banning Company
Paul Muchnick, Art Director, Paul Muchnick Company
Len Miller, Marketing Director, Copy Group Advertising
Tyger Gilbert, Creative Director, Gilbert Advertising Ltd.
Karen Deluca, Art Director, David H. Block Advertising, Inc.
J. Dietz, Art Director, J.M. Kesslinger & Associates
Ellie Malivis, Vice-Pres/Creative Dir. Metzdorf-Marschalk
Robert Bator, Robert Bator & Associates

Advertising agencies:
Needham, Harper & Steers, Inc.
Foote, Cone & Belding/Honig
J. Walter Thompson Company
Hill Holliday Connors Cosmopulos, Inc.
Greenstone & Rabasca Advertising
Elving Johnson Advertising, Inc.
John Crowe Advertising Agency
Fillman Advertising, Inc.
Caldwell/Van Riper Advertising/Public Relations
Quinlan, Keene, Peck & McShay, Inc.
KSK Communications, Ltd.
Evans Wyatt Advertising

Special thanks for use of artwork:
Mrs. John Held, Jr.
Ken Hull, Boalsburg, State College, PA
T.M. Orr

States represented by advertising agencies:

Arizona	Michigan
California	Nebraska
Illinois	New Jersey
Iowa	New Mexico
Louisiana	New York
Maryland	Texas
Massachusetts	Virginia